"Bon Courage, Les Anglais.
(Tales of the Uninitiated in Rural France)

By

Peter & Christine Wakefield

Illustrated by Fifi Sharplin

Copyright © Peter & Christine Wakefield 2012

Peter & Christine Wakefield assert the moral right to be identified as the authors of this work

ISBN 978-1-291-06418-6

www.publishnation.co.uk

All rights reserved. No part of this publication may be reproduced, stored in a retrieval system, or transmitted in any form or by any means, electronic, manual, photocopying, recording or otherwise, without the prior permission of the author.

This book is sold subject to the condition that it shall not, by way of trade or otherwise, be lent, re-sold, hired out or otherwise circulated, without the author's prior consent in any form of binding or cover other than that in which it is published and without a similar condition including this condition being imposed on the subsequent purchase.

"Bon Courage, Les Anglais."

(Tales of the Uninitiated in Rural France)

Contents.

1. Preface.

2. Quiet Miracles.

3. A Toast to Albert.

4. I don't think a wheelbarrow should be going this fast.

5. "'Snow Joke!"

6. Pooh là là.

7. Happiness is a wardrobe slowly rising in the air.

8. It's a dog's life

9. Whatever you do, don't let go of the rope!

10. "Henri, porte la table!"

11. Lessons learned the hard way.

12. Acknowledgements.

Preface

Daylight breaks again. The first brilliant rays of sunshine spread across the horizon. Down the valley the morning mist, covering the land, begins to rise, giving an almost eerie atmosphere.

We open our window to the sounds of the birds chattering and the cows, shrouded in the mist, lowing as they move across the fields. All else is tranquil. Morning vista in a small hamlet outside Bénévent L'Abbaye in rural France.

Welcome to "Bon Courage Les Anglais", where we seek to "open the shutter" to allow a glimmer of light to shine on the life of those who live there.

We were two uninitiated "Anglais"; Christine, who could fortunately speak almost fluent French, and Peter, who initially struggled to string a sentence together. Our little book chronicles the many heart-warming, often funny, sometimes life-changing experiences that we and our French neighbours shared together. They record the ups and downs, the achievements and heartbreaks, the triumphs and mistakes of those incredible years. They seek to share the everyday acts of neighbourliness, kindness and practical support, and the love that underpinned all of these. They show a way of life echoing shades of fifty years ago, that we look back on nostalgically here in England.

It was a deliberate decision to change the names of all those who appear in the book, French and English, to protect their identity. They are very special people to whom we will always owe a debt of gratitude. We have not changed the name of the location, Bénévent L'Abbaye, as this was already identified in the award-winning story, "Happiness is a wardrobe slowly rising in the air".

We fully accept that the personal insights we have described obviously relate to one small location in central France. We would not ever wish to claim that these are true for the whole of the country. Nevertheless, we are confident that many of them could probably be shared by "les autres Anglais" across France.

As you will discover, we were often wished "Bon Courage" by our French neighbours. This little phrase is very difficult to translate literally. It implies both "We wish you good luck in your undertaking" and "We admire your guts in taking on the task in the first place".

As you set out on the journey of reading through these stories we would also like to wish you all "Bon Courage" and genuinely hope you don't find the "task" too onerous!

Peter and Christine Wakefield

12th August 2012.

Quiet Miracles

It had been a long, hot and taxing trip down through France to our gîte at Pompadour, a beautiful town in Corrèze, home to one of the largest horse-riding centres in Europe. This journey was, for us, a baptism by fire; getting used to driving on the right, contending with the gridlocked streams of tourists heading south on the A20 on their annual pilgrimage in search of the sun. We struggled with trying to interpret French road signs and navigate our route through a strange and totally unfamiliar road system. It was with great relief, and utter exhaustion, that we finally reached our destination.

After a year of intensive research and frequent disagreements in England, we had narrowed our pursuit to find a holiday home to the Limousin/Poitou-Charentes region, and we had booked viewing appointments with three separate estate agencies in Bourganeuf, Rochechouart and Brive After a comfortable night and a mouth-watering breakfast of freshly baked croissants with creamy butter and home-made cherry jam, and a pot of delicious coffee, we set off for the town of Bourganeuf, filled with excitement and anticipation, to meet the first agent immobilier who had promised to show us three properties in the area.

It was a simple fifty-fifty choice; use the motorway again, which would be mind-numbingly boring, and looked much further on the map, or travel across country, using predominantly "D" roads. We decided to take the second option, following our trusty "Atlas routier." It took less than a quarter of an hour to realise that this was going to be the slower route by far. The scenery was breath-taking, set against a backdrop of vivid blue skies. The narrow roads twisted and turned up and down hills, through sleepy villages, beside babbling brooks, past fields of Limousin and Charollais cattle and through sun-dappled woods. This route became a test of nerve, however, negotiating sharp bends and trying to avoid deep ruts and pot holes in the road.

"Do you realise, we've just driven for half an hour without seeing another car?"

"Why did I open my big mouth!"

Round the very next bend we met a huge delivery lorry, head-on, in a single-track lane with no passing places, and, being chicken, we had to reverse to the last crossroads, trying not to end up ignominiously in the ditch. We then followed an ancient tractor, crawling along at a snail's pace and spewing out thick black fumes into the pure country air, for at least a mile. The journey was just like an obstacle course, made even worse by the constant blind spots resulting from being in a right-hand-drive vehicle, often having to rely on the judgement of the "eyes" sitting in the passenger seat ("Is it safe to overtake yet?").

Moreover, many of the T-junctions were lacking road signs, so it was matter of pure guesswork and trusting our instincts as to which general direction to take. We eventually tore up to the estate agent's office about half an hour late, panicking because of our ingrained English attitude to punctuality. Our fears proved groundless. Our agent, Marie, was gentle and gracious and, observing our frantic red faces, suggested having a coffee in the village square before setting off on our quest.

As we flopped down in relief at a table outside the bar-tabac, sheltered from the intense early-afternoon sun by a brightly coloured parasol, and with a strong black espresso in front of us, we slowly began to unwind.

"This is what we've been looking forward to all year!" we told Marie.

And suddenly everything felt different. There was a simple magic to the whole ethos and ambience of this little place. It was so peaceful, so tranquil, with locals sipping their "pastis" or "verre de rouge" and engaging in relaxed conversation. The slower pace of life was almost tangible. This memory was to stay with us for a long time to come. Over the years, many friends who came out for holidays also perceived the easy going, laid-back atmosphere in the French countryside.

We sat discussing the three viewings with Marie, and she said there was no need to rush off as we would easily get round all three properties within an afternoon. We eventually set off on our voyage of discovery, little realising how the next four hours would change our lives forever.

We knew, as soon as we set foot in the first two houses, that they were not right for us. At the first cottage we asked, "And where is the garden?". Marie indicated a postage-stamp parcel of land, on the opposite side of the road.

"We want somewhere to sit outside and have a barbecue, big enough for the grandchildren to go out and play when they are over" we declared. "This garden is just too small."

On to the second house. This had magnificent outbuildings and an oak-beamed barn, but was totally devoid of charm, being semi-derelict, with rat droppings in every room. Looking out onto a three-storey terrace of village houses, what could have been a stunning view was totally obscured by rural real estate. We might as well have been at home in Birmingham!

We were, by now, somewhat dispirited as we headed towards the third and final property, situated in a small hamlet outside Bénévent L'Abbaye. On paper this one seemed even less promising than the others. The photo showed a small dowdy-looking "maison de village," in a state of obvious neglect, whose front door opened straight onto the street outside. "Far too dangerous for the grandchildren," we agreed. It was described as two-bedroomed, with a large garden and two outbuildings.

"Just take a look," Marie suggested. " you may be pleasantly surprised!"

"Unlikely" we both thought, uncharitably. "Perhaps we should have upped the budget after all!"

When we went in through the front door to the main living space, the sight that greeted us had to be seen to be believed. It was dark and dingy; there was damp seeping up through the floors; wires and electric cables hung everywhere; soot covered the main walls, and the oak-beamed ceiling was blackened by smoke from the open fire that had discoloured it over many years.

"It will need one or two things doing to it" Marie ventured. Understatement of the year! It would need total renovation, and that was not on our agenda. We wanted somewhere we could come to for rest and relaxation. A modicum of decoration would be fine, but not a full-scale refurbishment.

At the rear of the house, there was a heavy old wooden door with a frosted glass top section which prevented us seeing out into the garden. Marie unlocked it with a huge rusty key and there was loud creaking as it slowly opened. We wandered out onto a small patio.

As we stepped outside, we both stood rooted to the spot.

"This must be one of the most beautiful views in the whole of France!" Chris gasped. The long, overgrown garden ran down to a boundary wall that dropped away into a field below. The field sloped gently down into a lush, green valley. In the dip, beside a small stream, a herd of Limousin cattle were grazing lazily. The far side of the valley rose majestically towards the story-book skyline of Bénévent, with its hotch-potch of stone houses nestling close to the twelfth-century Abbey.

We had come from the frantic pace and incessant noise of inner-city Birmingham to a small piece of rural paradise. Here we were experiencing total calm, peace and tranquillity as we drank in the vibrant green countryside spread out before us. Even the road it was situated on was a cul-de-sac, with only two houses beyond. We both knew straight away that we had fallen in love with this little house, uninhabitable as it was, and that beyond all doubt this was the retreat we had dreamed of. Despite this realisation, we were determined not to rush into things and, shortly afterwards, we set off back to Pompadour, this time prudently taking the "autoroute".

However, by 9.00 a.m. the next morning, back in the comfort of our gîte, we were dialling the immobilier, and asking Marie to put in an offer on the Bénévent property. We could not believe we had found such a treasure in such a short time. It was nothing short of a miracle.

We had both fallen for this little house but, even then, we could not let our hearts rule our heads. The foundations might be playing host to an army of termites, and the rafters riddled with death-watch beetle. Through an English contact, Colin, via the estate agency, we arranged for a builder to meet us at the house the following day and give it a thorough inspection.

Back up the motorway again.

Colin and his builder friend, Paul, were waiting for us as we pulled up at the house and, after the customary greetings, the survey began. When Paul went round to the back garden, he stopped dead and turning to us, exclaimed, "What an incredible view!" He went over every nook and cranny of both the house and the two outbuildings.

"What's that crack in the kitchen wall?" Peter enquired tentatively.

"Nothing to worry about! Look at the foundation stones, perfectly in line, no lifting at all. The structure is solid, and the roof is in good condition. I can see no reason whatsoever why you shouldn't go ahead and buy". We could have hugged him but we settled for a hearty handshake and profuse thanks.

Colin accompanied us inside before leaving. We noticed he seemed slightly restless, and we hoped he wasn't going to disagree with Paul's opinion.

Addressing the two of us, he spoke very quietly. "This place has been empty for two-and-a-half years, and lots of people have been to look at it, but rejected it for various reasons. I can't explain what I'm going to say next, but at this moment in time, I feel, deep-down, that this house has been waiting for you."

"I know exactly what you mean" Peter replied. "We sensed that as well. It's like a quiet miracle's happening for us".

Just a few days later, accompanied by Marie, we had the privilege of meeting the owner of the property, Monsieur Duclos. We loved his gentleness, his sense of humour, and the quiet dignity he displayed as he related the story of the house to us. It had been in his family, along with two others in the hamlet, for generations. In the last twenty years it had been rented out to an elderly French couple, both of whom had passed away. The family now felt it was the right time to sell.

At the end of the meeting, he accompanied us out into the street and held out his hand.

As we shook it he said, "I'm delighted to sell the house to you, and wish you every happiness here for the future". He then went back to his car and drove away. Up to this point we had hardly seen the neighbours, but on one side we had an elderly French couple, Solange and Gaston. Dressed in blue dungarees, check shirt and flat cap, walking stick in hand, Gaston ambled up the road to meet us, having seen the handshake.

Marie, who was still with us, happened to mention that there were other potential buyers showing interest in the house, in particular a couple from Paris. This produced a moment of panic in us.

"Could we be gazumped now, because that happens all the time in England?" Chris wanted to know.

Gaston shook his head. "No, not a chance. The owner has given you his word and sealed it by shaking hands. Terminé. The deal is complete. He will not go back on his word. That's the tradition here. That's the way we do things and that's the way they have always been done."

We felt all our fears and concerns drain away. Another quiet miracle.

But there was still one more remarkable event to come that, in its unique way, made us even more deeply aware that buying a "résidence secondaire" in rural France was the right decision.

We had travelled all the way across France in our battered old Peugeot 205, which had already been round the clock, though, admittedly, it had never given us the slightest trouble up until now. Chris was praying for it to be confined to the scrapheap and replaced by a super-duper shiny new Mégane, with an actual, working suspension system.

"They don't build them like this any more", Peter would invariable reply. "There's plenty of life in the old girl yet!"

Heading back to Pompadour after the meeting with Monsieur Duclos, we had just reached the town and were turning the corner into the long, winding road leading to our gîte when, without any warning, the car coasted to a complete stop. We tried to get a response from the clutch and gears but nothing happened. It was by now very late in the day, and all the local garages had long closed.

"Merde! Quelle catastrophe! What on earth were we going to do?"

Then, in a house across the road, a door opened and a young Frenchman came over to us.

"Got a problem, monsieur?" he asked, "I'm on holiday here with my parents, but I'm from Paris, and I'm a mechanic."

We just didn't believe it. Of all the places to break down and it had happened outside the home of a mechanic "en vacances". He lifted the bonnet and studied the engine. After only a couple of minutes of pulling things and checking things he looked up at us and smiled. "Nothing too serious. The coupling bar has broken where one end has sheared off. That's all".

We had never heard of a coupling bar, so would never have known where to look for it. "How do we get a replacement?" we asked.

"These parts are easy to come by" he replied. "There are plenty of Peugeot garages round here. I can easily take you to find one tomorrow when they open. Leave the car here. It will be perfectly safe." With that, he helped us to push the forlorn vehicle onto the grass verge, bid us "Au revoir" and crossed to the house.

The next morning he ended up driving us to three garages. The first, unfortunately, didn't have the part in stock, so off we went. The second had it in stock and wanted to charge fifteen euros for it, which we thought was great. This was the moment we were introduced to the French art of haggling.

"C'est trop cher" our mechanic protested, and there then followed a very lively, quick-fire exchange of words and much gesticulating of arms.

"No, no! Fifteen euros is fine if that's all it costs to get us back to England again." Needless to say, we left without the part.

The third garage also had the required coupling in stock and once again we stood back and admired the inevitable ritual of prolonged haggling, this time involving a great deal of banter mixed with good-natured but hard negotiation. The show concluded with a brisk handshake, confirming the knock-down price of five euros.

We drove back to our car, and within two minutes the repair was finished.

"Ça y est," said our friend, dropping the bonnet. He refused to accept anything for his time and labour, waving to us as we drove away and wishing us all the best with the house purchase and "bon courage".

In a period of just under two weeks, we had come to France and bought what could loosely be described as our dream "résidence secondaire". By the Christmas of that year (2002) we became the legal owners of a French property.

"Yes," we agreed, "miracles really can happen."

A Toast to Albert

Over the following eighteen months French workmen installed new plumbing, electrics and central heating in our new holiday home. By the summer of 2004 most of the major rebuilding work had been completed and we were able to enjoy two glorious weeks there.

It had been one of the hottest days of the holiday, and one we had set aside for two simple tasks. All morning we had been working to remove some ancient green flock wallpaper in one of the upstairs bedrooms. Success was being measured by scraping off a six-inch square every hour. This revoltingly awful patterned paper must have been glued on with some unknown type of old French superglue.

We had brought a wallpaper steamer from England and we tried this for half an hour. It didn't loosen any wallpaper but it sure made it look clean. By lunchtime we had scraped off a miniscule area of about two foot by two foot. Three hours of strenuous work!

Well, there was only one thing for it: - a baguette lunch on the patio under the shade of the parasol, washed down with a glass of chilled Chardonnay. Reflection on a problem is always a good idea, especially when it happens during "le déjeuner".

How to solve the wallpaper problem? Stop stripping. No, not us, the paper off the walls! Instead, purchase some large cans of tough, gloopy exterior wall paint when we were back in England, bring them back on our next trip, and slap it over the offending paper. The reason for this export/import operation was that French paint tends to be somewhat on the thin side and it would probably take five to six coats to cover these walls. (We did bring the paint over the following Easter, and it did the job brilliantly.)

So back to that afternoon. The next thrilling challenge was to knock down the breeze-block structure built slap-bang outside our back door, just a few feet from our patio, totally obscuring the idyllic view. This job would have to be tackled in temperatures of thirty-eight to forty degrees.

Peter had emptied it the previous week, taking out old buckets, a pair of vintage wellingtons still emitting a quite unique pong, and an old rusty garden fork with two prongs missing. The only other mysterious item was a long, rough-hewn oak plank, blackened in places, with a round hole in the centre. Through lack of knowledge of the need to handle old planks with gloves, Peter was introduced to some particularly nasty French pests – the "aoûtats".

It is likely that most people will have never heard of "aoûtats". They are harvest mite parasites that live in old timber, and also in overhanging branches of trees, usually in late August and early September. They cunningly drop onto your skin and then make themselves at home by burrowing. Within a short time of the first contact they produce itchy red blotches all over the arms and body.

The result is that you have an overwhelming need to scratch everywhere, which only makes it worse. Our pharmacist told us that antihistamine tablets might help to reduce the initial itchiness, but there is no real treatment that will stop them – you have to wait until they drop off or expire. Aaaagh! The joys of country life!

The time had now come to demolish the structure. We picked up the sledgehammer and were just about to make a start when a voice hollered.

"Un moment! Attendez!" (Wait)

It was old Gaston, our French neighbour. He ambled across the top garden, wearing his trade-mark denim dungarees and beloved blue cap.

"This was old Albert's toilet" he said, chuckling to himself.

"He always had to come out here" He laughed. "The old dragon wouldn't allow him to use the toilet in the house. Every day for the last ten years of his life he had to come out here, whatever the weather. He used to dread the bitter winter mornings because his bum nearly froze to the seat!"

He looked at the sledgehammer.

"Vous permettez?" he said. "Can I strike the first blow for old Albert's sake?"

"Certainement" we replied.

As the hammer head hit the wall and the first block smashed into pieces he let out a great whoop of joy. It was clearly a moment of triumph. He put down the hammer, gave us a thumbs-up, and ambled back home.

"Merveilleux" we heard him muttering as he crossed the garden.

As we took a good look at the breeze blocks we were hit by a brainwave. We knew we were going to build a new wood store and needed a solid base. If we could knock out the breeze blocks one by one we could reuse them to lay the base.

What a brilliant idea!

We went to the garage and brought back some chisels and lump hammers. One hour later, after chiselling away at the mortar we had finally managed to remove two breeze blocks. We estimated that to do the rest would take about three months and plenty of bad language. The idea was now not feeling quite so brilliant.

The problem was the mortar, though this is the wrong word for it. The genius who had built this little gem had wanted to make sure it never fell down, and had used concrete instead of mortar between the blocks.

We were just saying "Oh dear", or words to that effect, kicking the breeze-blocks in frustration, when a passing French neighbour, seeing us looking fed up, hot and bothered, strolled down the garden.

"Qu'est-ce qu'il y a, mes amis?" he asked.

We should perhaps have taken a little more time to explain what we had been trying to do.

"We're trying to knock the wall down".

"I can help if you want".

"Great" we said, "Go ahead".

He was only a small man but must have had enormous strength in his arms, because he took the sledgehammer and smashed it heavily at the base of the blocks and, as it made contact, the entire side wall shattered.

He swung again at the base of the second wall. Ditto. The remaining wall standing now looked distinctly unsafe. He simply pulled the top of it, and, as we jumped back, it collapsed onto the ground.

"Eh voilà!"

Looking at a great heap of rubble now, with not a single breeze block remaining intact, we thanked him for all his help, stressing how much we appreciated it. Another great idea bites the dust!

In the early evening Gaston returned to view our handiwork, and knocked on the door. We all went together down to the heap.

"Albert would have loved to have been here to savour this moment" he said.

The occasion called for a celebratory drink. Glasses of ice-cold beer fitted the bill perfectly. We sat together on the patio surveying the pile.

Gaston made the toast as the three of us raised glasses; -

"To the memory of Albert! May he now finally rest in peace".

I don't think a wheelbarrow should be going this fast

The time had now come on our plan of works to install the gas tank that would supply our central heating system. This was going to be buried in the top garden. Mains gas had unfortunately not yet reached this part of the Creuse.

"It's here! It's here!" Being only five years old, this was for Laurent, our neighbour's son, a great occasion. Wow! He'd never seen anything like this before.

Trundling down the road in front of his house was a JCB digger, bearing, on heavy chains, an enormous gas tank. Being in a tiny hamlet with very tight access, we had notified our immediate neighbours of the impending delivery scheduled for the end of siesta, and "eh voilà" here it was, dead on time.

It took only a short time for the news to spread, using one of the most effective communications systems ever invented - the French rural hamlet bush telegraph system. Word flew from neighbour to neighbour, house to house. By the time the digger had reached the gate into our top garden, local families were already congregating to watch the proceedings.

Getting down from his cab, Serge, the driver, introduced himself and walked around the site studying the paperwork provided by the gas company, pacing out the ground with reassuring savoir-faire.

As the operation began, we could only marvel at his skill and expertise. He started by deftly depositing the huge tank over the garden wall. Then, as there was only a narrow access gate into our garden, having disposed of his load he began to manoeuvre his JCB through the seemingly impossible gap.

Forward; reverse; forward; reverse; left hand down a bit; right hand down a bit. Within a matter of seconds the digger was passing between our stone gateposts. As he cleared the entrance with only a few centimetres clearance on either side, there was an admiring flurry of applause from the swelling band of onlookers.

However, there was yet another obstacle to impede his progress. Just a couple of metres inside the gate the previous owners of our property had constructed a brick barbecue which rested on a large concrete slab. Our trusty digger driver got down from his machine and studied the barbecue carefully, stroking his chin in deep reflection. Scrambling back into the cab, he started the engine and lowered the pronged bucket, advancing until it just touched the edge of the base.

Then, very delicately he proceeded, inch by inch, (or should that be centimetre by centimetre?) to nudge the barbecue across the grass until he had just sufficient space to turn into the garden. Not one brick had been dislodged or damaged. A further enthusiastic burst of applause and congratulatory chorus of "Bravo!" What appeared to be an impossible task to us laymen was, to our expert, the ideal opportunity to demonstrate what a skilled and accomplished French workman, in total command of his machinery, can achieve.

He then proceeded to dig a hole- a very big hole. It was so big that, if we had had the time, we could have held a party in it and invited all the onlookers for aperitifs (as one tends to do in rural France)

Now, you may, or may not, be asking yourself, "What did they do with all the earth that was displaced from the hole?" (It was ninety per cent clay and boulders just below the surface soil).

Well, we had a brainwave. Our top garden was two metres higher than our bottom garden, separated by a dry stone wall. We needed something to connect the two.

"Dump all the soil over the wall. We're going to build a ramp" we said confidently. Serge did as we suggested, and by the time the hole was dug we had a huge mound of clay and rubble in place, to construct our fantastic new ramp. He finished the operation with a flamboyant flourish by using the heavy bucket to compact all the rocks and clay, providing a flat top to our ramp to further cheers from the gathered crowd.

Hoisting the tank aloft, he advanced towards the crater, lowering it down slowly. Would it fit? No measurements had been taken during the entire operation. And, of course, it fitted perfectly. He then proceeded to scoop up the remaining soil to bury all but the surface hatch and lid, patting the earth down gently with the bottom of his bucket. He even spread some strips of weedy turf he had set to one side delicately over the flattened surface, surveying the finished task with pride. We expressed our grateful thanks and appreciation for a job well done.

Finally, having filled in the necessary forms in triplicate and with the customary hearty handshakes all round, Serge and his co-driver departed, with a cheery "Bon après-midi, Mesdames, Messieurs", and a theatrical bow.

Incredible! We now had the tank buried, with the added bonus of a new ramp only needing minimal work to complete. It was a moment to savour and, the show being over, we bid a fond farewell to all our neighbours and several spectators we had never seen before.

So what about the barbecue? How did it get moved back into place? Well, to be honest, it didn't. It just sat there in the garden, lost and forlorn. One of our French friends, Guy, valiantly tried to move it with a chain attached to the bumper of his ancient Renault 5. Loud revving of the engine, clouds of black smoke, spinning back wheels and an encyclopaedic torrent of expletive, but it still wouldn't budge! The ruts Guy's tyres left in the garden remained there for months.

Many suggestions were made about what to do about the marooned barbecue, and numerous glasses of Burgundy were imbibed whilst pondering on the problem. We eventually came up with the only logical solution. Just hit it with a big hammer! We did, and it fell to pieces. And, of course, that also called for a celebratory drink or two.

So now we come to the central focus of this particular story. The Ramp! It took us only a few hours to flatten the surface and ensure that all the rocks were covered with compacted clay. It was now ready for use.

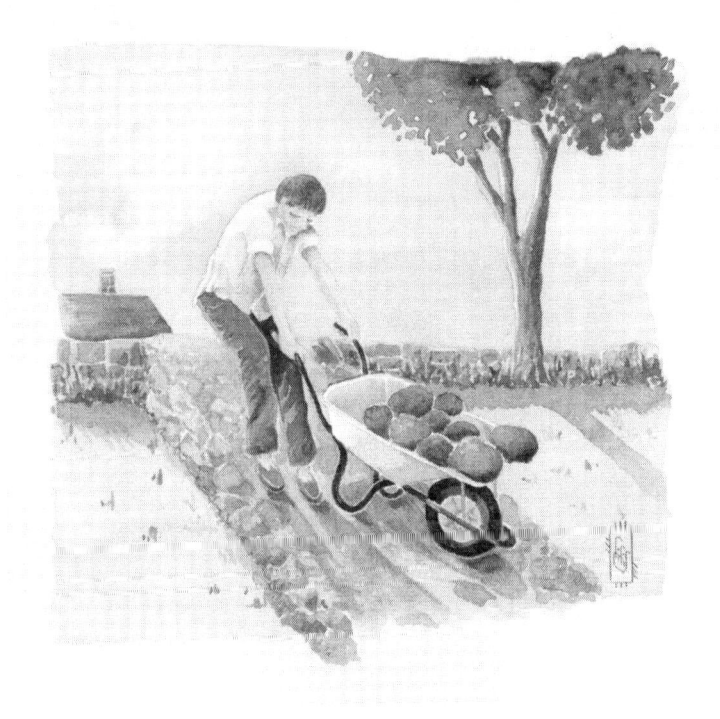

We well remember that fateful day. We brought out our wheelbarrow and loaded it with some rocks that we intended to use to make a rockery in the bottom garden. Big mistake! In fact, massive mistake!

All was well while Peter and the wheelbarrow went over the flat surface at the top and stepped onto the ramp. From then on it went downhill all the way – quite literally, at an incredible speed. He remembered the moment our "brouette" started hurtling down the ramp at mach one and was saying to himself, "I don't think a wheelbarrow should be going this fast". Near the bottom, and still gathering momentum, he had no option but to let go. The barrow lurched to a halt. Unfortunately the contents didn't. Rocks catapulted all over the veggie patch flattening everything in sight.

However, he was not going to be beaten! Picking himself up and dusting himself down, he collected the wheelbarrow and loaded it with a couple of bags of garden waste. You would think he'd have learned on the way down. He started to push it up the ramp, taking extreme care, and going slowly, and then more slowly, until finally, two-thirds of the way up, it came to a grinding halt. The acute angle of the ramp defeated him. He could push no further.

There was a law of science here somewhere. It begins with "Never stop on a steep incline". He was still clutching the handles as the wheel went into reverse mode and he and the barrow slipped slowly but gracefully back down the ramp.

This is the moment when you know you've made two grave mistakes.

The first was getting the slope of the ramp completely wrong. The second, which was to have far more long-term consequences, was not having the foresight to get all the clay and boulders taken away by the contractor.

So, to finish this story, we had to dismantle the entire ramp, bit by bit, stone by stone, boulder by boulder, by filling buckets and emptying them one at a time into our trailer to take to the local tip. Hundreds and hundreds of buckets! Trip after trip with the trailer going to the tip so often that the site manager there became quite a friend who hailed us on every visit, "Peter, Christine, encore!" (This literally translated means "again" but with the emphasis he put on the word it was probably more accurately translated as "not you two idiots again!") During one of the last trips, he called us over and said we had become such valued visitors he was thinking of making us honorary site members.

Another failed challenge to put down to experience! Another steep learning curve (and this one certainly was steep!) But it had seemed like such a good idea at the time. "C'est la vie"!

"'Snow joke!"

Another learning curve was just around the corner. We had now moved permanently to France, and were for the first time in the Limousin in the heart of winter. The activities of summer are now a distant memory. The streets, once so vibrant, so full of colour are empty, deserted and grey.

It had been a day of celebration when we signed the initial documents to purchase our little house, intended as a holiday retreat, in the summer of 2002. It didn't seem important then, that it nestled at the bottom of our little hamlet, accessed by three small roads, all with steep gradients. Aha!

Did we think about that access in the middle of winter? In a word – no. But we sure did once we had moved in. On frosty December mornings these same sloping roads would be white-covered by the night frost, and could remain frozen-over all day. Picturesque, until you want to drive out.

One very memorable morning, having slipped over on the icy surface twice just walking across to our garage we decided that it was not safe to take the car out. A little later Marcel knocked on our door.

"Just driving up to the shops if there's anything you need?" ("Up" being the operative word.)

"A baguette would be great" we replied, "thanks a lot".

As we closed the door, we looked again at the white-covered tarmac and thought "there is a brave man". We heard him start the engine in his garage, and couldn't help peeping out of our window. We watched him reverse his car out and onto the slope. We saw the red of his rear lights as he applied his brakes. Then, slowly his car began to slip backwards. There was no grip, no traction whatsoever. As we ran out of the door the car continued to slip down the slope, coming to a halt just inches from his house. There was nothing we could have done to stop it. We ran to the boot and pushed very hard but it was far too heavy.

"Yvette!" we shouted, "we need some help".

She came out and, seeing our struggle, joined us in the pushing. All to no avail.

With possibly a slight sense of embarrassment, but certainly with a broad beaming smile Marcel got out of the car. It was obvious that it could not be pushed back up the slope, but it was blocking the road. Peter said "Sacrebleu! What are we going to do?" A short discussion ensued and the solution was simple. Call the farmer. If in trouble in the winter, call the farmer.

A few minutes later, Bernard came chugging down the road on his tractor. When he arrived he looked at all of us. He came over and gave each of us a cheery embrace. He took the towing chain from the tractor and attached it to the car. Then very slowly he pulled it up the slope as we took a corner each to ensure that it wouldn't slide sideways. Very soon it was level with the garage and we all pushed it around so that it could be driven in safely.

Success! The car safely away and no injury to anyone. Merveilleux!

It was too early really for drinks so we all headed indoors for a cup of strong black coffee. In just one cup there might have been a tad of whisky added but we will never know. However there were still no baguettes.

"I know," I said to Chris," why don't you walk up to the boulangerie? The exercise will do you good."

"I tell you what," she replied, "why don't we both go, and then the exercise will do us both good!" From the tone of the reply I was unsure if this was said in the form of a request or a command. We both went up to town.

When we read of other people's experiences of their French neighbours and problems that they encountered, we were thankful for the support, care and real love we felt on so many occasions. There was one particular week that will always be etched on our memories. It was the end of January 2007, and mid-way through our first winter there.

In the late afternoon there was a shout over our wall from our neighbour, Marcel, who warned us that there could be some heavy snow falls through the night. Heeding the advice we put our car away, locking the large old oak doors for the night.

The following morning when we awoke we sensed immediately that something was wrong. The bedroom felt much colder than it should have done, as our central heating had always been very effective. We were unable to turn on the bedside light. We tried the main lights and, again, nothing. We had lost our electricity supply.

We knew at once that this meant we had also lost our central heating, as the pilot light was electrically generated.

We looked out of the bedroom window onto the garden and it had been buried under a huge blanket of snow. We gaped open-mouthed. We could not believe that so much snow had fallen in such a short time. We knew that we were facing serious problems.

Aware of the cold in the house, we dressed as quickly as possible in our warmest clothing and went downstairs. It was imperative that we lit the wood-burner. We always kept some kindling beside the fire, and enough logs for the day. Within a few minutes it was starting to blaze and there was a reassuring roar in the chimney as smoke began to billow upwards. The heat being given out felt quite comforting as the cast iron stove gradually got hotter and hotter. Our next challenge was to try to work out some plan of action for the rest of the day and evening.

One immediate requirement was to find every candle we possessed. We would need these through the long night-time hours. More importantly we would need them to go to the bathroom, as this was a room with no windows. The good news was that we had kept a couple in the drawer of our buffet in case of emergencies. The bad news was that we had left all the rest in our outbuilding across the road.

We decided we had better fetch some across, and unlocked the front door. This was the precise moment when we knew that something in excess of fifty centimetres of snow now blocked our road. To make matters worse it had drifted to a much greater height against the garage and outhouse doors, having been driven against them by the wind.

With great difficulty we struggled through the drifts to the outbuilding door. This was when we realised that the scout motto "be prepared" would have been wise to have heeded weeks before. Our need was simple – a shovel or a spade. I asked Chris "Are you sure that they're both in the outhouse, or could they be in the back garden?"

"No" she replied", I remember putting them away a few days ago".

With both of them in the outbuilding we needed something to dig with. Back to the house to search around. Eventually we came up with the nearest thing we could find to a spade. This was the roasting tin with a lid from the oven. It took nearly half an hour and a lot of energy using our implements to clear sufficient snow to allow us to wrench the outhouse door open a fraction. Squeezing inside, we found the shovel and spade and our collection of candles. A minor success.

We went back indoors to thaw out. We now had enough candles, but realised we didn't have enough logs. And the log pile was tucked up safely inside the garage.

"Look on the bright side," Chris said, "this time we at least have a shovel". I couldn't really describe how much comfort those words brought!

One hour later we had shifted sufficient snow away from the garage door to allow it to be opened to give access to the logs. There was no way that they could be transported across the snow. We hatched a cunning plan- throw and catch. One of us stood outside the house door as the catcher and stacker.

The other was the thrower. You learn very fast to judge both the distance to throw a log and the speed needed. In a little under an hour we had a large stack in the house.

Coffee-time was very welcome. We wondered how our friends were coping, and if they had had the same amount of snow. We picked up the telephone to dial. The line was dead. No telephone.

Our thoughts turned to our neighbours, especially Solange further down our road. She was now a widow and lived alone. We dug out a path to her front door and knocked. When she opened it we were hit by the warmth coming from her kitchen. She had kept burning wood all night so her downstairs rooms were lovely and warm.
"Come in," she said, "you both look frozen".

We had lost the use of all our modern media equipment so we had no way of listening to the news. Not so Solange. There in her kitchen was one of the most ancient battery-operated radios we have ever seen. This was clearly broadcasting local news about the effects of the snowfall.
"It's not looking good" she said, "the power is down all over the area and all telephone lines have been cut by the weight of the snow that fell on them. It looks like it will be several days before anyone will be able to get to us".

No telephone either. Our hearts sank. No heat, no power, no telephone. We think she must have read our thoughts. "Don't worry" she said, seeking to reassure us, "we'll all pull together and we will get through this". Then she asked us "Is there anything I can do for you?" This offer really touched us as we had called on her to offer our help and instead she was offering us support.

"I'm sure we'll manage" Peter replied, and having checked that she had everything she needed, we struggled back to the house.

As we got in, and thinking of life with no telephone, I asked Chris "Where's the mobile?"
"In the buffet drawer" she answered. "It just needs charg...." Her voice tailed off. With a sinking feeling we got it out of the drawer and turned it on. Flat as a pancake!

Later that morning we began to experience the love and care from neighbours in our hamlet. There was a loud knock on the door and the farmer stood there with a freshly baked baguette which he had collected from the boulanger on his tractor. Just after mid-day another neighbour delivered a bowl of piping hot soup, as they were concerned we might not have been able to cook. These simple loving acts touched us deeply.

By late afternoon it was already getting dark and our downstairs room was looking cosy with the candles burning and the glow coming from the opened wood-burner. This first evening had a sense of excitement and the unknown about it. We enjoyed a vegetable stew which we had cooked in our Le Creuset cast-iron pot on the hot- plate of the wood-burner. We had had the foresight, when our cooker was installed, to have an electric oven and gas hob. The hob now allowed us the luxury of boiling water. At least we could have a wash in hot water.

The next morning gave rise to new challenges. The temperature had dropped to minus 18 degrees in the night, and this had frozen the surface of the snow, making any walking through the paths we had cleared quite dangerous. Our serious concern now was for all the food in our large chest freezer, which we had filled for the winter. We mentioned this to

Marcel who told us that, if we didn't lift the lid, everything would be safe for the first twenty-four hours.

About an hour later, we heard what we thought at first was the noise of an engine but we realised this was impossible. Venturing outside we saw that the farmer had delivered a generator to Marcel, with a second extension cable to connect to our freezer. He said we could have the use of the generator for an hour each morning and evening. Once again we were really indebted for this help.

We were then given a tip by Marcel to help prolong the life of the freezer contents which we would never have thought of in a million years, "Fill some carrier bags with snow and put them inside the top of the freezer." Obvious, when you think about it!

We were learning just how our neighbours had managed to adapt to the harsh winters.

Chris volunteered to walk up into the town to collect essential supplies for our hamlet. Setting off up the slope she was cocooned in a bizarre, mismatching assortment of woollies and waterproofs, with a huge rucksack slung on her back, and looked like Scott of the Antarctic.

Eventually she reached the supermarket which had, of course, also lost all its power and lighting. The assistants were trying everything in their means to serve the customers. They met them at the entrance door and wrote down their orders. Then, armed with torches, they went round the store, collecting the goods on the list. Hand-held calculators were used to tot up the bill and payment was only in cash. Even in the midst of adversity there was almost a Dunkirk spirit with everyone sharing accounts of their experiences while they waited. This was all light-hearted and good-natured, infused with a great deal of humour.

After her trek back and a welcome cup of coffee, Chris delivered everyone's orders. Although we did not realise it at the time, this help made a deep impression on our French neighbours.

By the evening of the second day it was becoming harder to keep going. Even the simple task of having any sort of wash meant carrying hot water from the cooker to the bathroom. Washing by candlelight was something we were adapting to. Going to the toilet by candlelight was a whole different experience!

Yvette came round the next morning with some news.
"I met Françoise at the top of the road," she said. "She told me that many elderly residents living in houses without wood-burners had found it impossible to stay in their homes".
"What's happened to them?" we asked.
"The Mairie has opened the Salle des Fêtes (the local community centre) as an emergency shelter, providing them all with food and accommodation".
It made our little struggles seem quite insignificant.

We heard later that some stalwart and intrepid elderly residents, with no proper heating, had braved it out in their own homes. They had wrapped themselves up in every item of clothing they possessed, woollies, heavy coats, thick socks, fur boots, and wrapped in blankets, had sat it out, getting by on cold rations supplemented by occasional hot meals supplied by friends and neighbours.

On the third morning there was a knock on the door.

"C'est moi." Solange sang out, and we ushered her in out of the cold. She had a large Carrefour bag in her hand.

"I've brought you something to eat." And with that she took a duck out of the bag. "I had four in the freezer, but that was really all, so I've decided to empty it. I'm giving away the ones I can't eat". We thanked her profusely.

That evening we had a delicious duck casserole which had been quietly simmering for hours on the wood-burner. The smell that filled our living room was something special. As we tucked in we raised a glass of wine for a toast.

"Salut Solange! Et bon appétit!"

In the midst of the difficulties there were moments of humour. We opened the back door to show our dog Ben the snow. Unaware of how deep it was, he bounded out into the thick of it. It was the last we saw of him for several minutes. We watched as a track appeared along the snow but no sign of the explorer. Then we heard a low whimpering and saw an abominable snowman on four legs coming slowly back towards us. The freezing snow had stuck all over his coat. He rushed inside and lay down in front of the wood-burner until his white overcoat had slowly melted away, spending some time sucking the ice out of his paws. Needless to say he didn't venture out again, apart from the odd super-fast toilet break.

On the fourth day, with the temperature still way below freezing, and no melting of the snow, we experienced what we still call our surreal moment. We were looking down over the back garden, and in the top right corner we saw our rotary washing line still covered in snow. We are not sure if it was the icy cold that made the tiniest bit of difference to the weight on its' line, but we watched as it slowly buckled and then bent over. For some reason, seeing it happen felt quite a sad moment and Chris said to me, "Well this feels like the end of the line!"

By the fifth day the atmosphere in our little hamlet became very heated whilst the temperature remained bitingly cold. Looking out of our window we saw all the lights come on in the town and realised that they had at last restored the electricity supply. "Great" we thought, "in a few minutes we should also be back on too". This expectation was very short-lived. The Mayor told us that, along with only a few other small hamlets, we would be the last houses to be reconnected. This news did not go down well.
"This is getting ridiculous," Peter declared. "'Snow joke!"

Some of our French neighbours walked up to the Town Hall to express their views about our situation very clearly. It must have had some impact. That afternoon a large tractor came down into the hamlet with a huge bucket on its front. It cleared one track of snow right through the road and then drove off. On the surface this may appear to have helped in some way. This "snow clearance", however, achieved the opposite effect to what was intended. It had still left frozen snow and ice lying on the road surface which made it a death-trap to walk on. More significantly, as it pushed the blanket of snow aside, it had banked up against the doors to all our garages and outbuildings. "Oh bother" we all said, or words to that effect, as we surveyed the task ahead, reaching for the shovels.

By now we were all feeling very exhausted and wearied from the challenge of just keeping going through each day. This made us all very disgruntled. Suffice it to say our feelings were communicated in no uncertain terms to the Town Hall.

On the morning of the seventh day we heard the sound of lorries at the top of the hamlet. Within two hours our electricity supply was reconnected, and that afternoon the telephone cabling was repaired. It was wonderful. "Let there be light" and there was light. Our boiler kicked back into life and the central heating came on. There was just such a sense of relief that we could begin to get back to some form of normality. We could even enjoy the luxury of a hot shower.

It took some considerable time for all the snow to melt and for it to become safe to use the roads again. A couple of days after the reconnection, a reporter from the local newspaper visited the hamlet, knowing how long we had been trapped in by the weather, to get an inside perspective from the residents. When his article appeared in the newspaper the following day we saw that the French locals had paid their personal tribute to "the two English" who had helped them so much over the week.

We cannot put into words how much we valued and appreciated these comments. The article stressed just how much everyone had pulled together and given each other both physical and moral support.

Yes, Solange had been right all along.

Pooh là là

The following spring, in early 2007 we were enjoying coffee with Chris's daughter Katherine, sitting out on the patio and watching the herd of Limousin cattle grazing lazily on the rolling hills. In just a few hours we would be taking her to the airport to fly back to England.

"I love it here", Katherine said. "It's just so peaceful and it been great to have these few days to relax and unwind".

She gazed down the garden and suddenly asked, "By the way, what's that funny grey stuff oozing out of the ground down by the raspberry canes?" "Funny grey stuff" on its own would not have been a concern. "Oozing out of the ground" can happen quite often after heavy downpours of rain, as small pools on the surface overflow. However the combination of the two together is not something you really want to think about.

"I'll go down and take a look" I said, remarking that I had not noticed a problem there before. As I approached the affected area a pungent smell invaded my nostrils. A distinctive, unmistakeable niff that I knew immediately could only be one thing. It had to be waste liquid from our "fosse septique" (septic tank).

When I got back to the house I remarked casually that it was really nothing to worry about, just some rotting vegetation that had collected in a small pool of water. But on the way back from the airport after seeing Katherine safely onto her flight, I broke the news to Chris about my worst suspicions about "the funny grey stuff".

Four years earlier, during our first summer vacation after buying the house, we had decided we needed to find the exact location of our fosse. This decision had come as a result of cordial table-talk with new-found English friends at our local hostelry. We had not met up with them more than two or three times before we discovered a peculiar phenomenon. When they met up and socialised, discussion never seemed to centre on the weather, football, or even the challenges of daily life in rural France. No! The hot topic of conversation was septic tanks; the unpredictable vagaries of the frequently malfunctioning, invariably blocked and permanently malodorous "fosse". Not the most savoury subject to accompany your "café-crème" and "pain au chocolat"!

We were very fortunate in having wonderful French neighbours who had been most welcoming to us, as English and decidedly "green" newcomers. Gaston, a retired smallholder, had already proved to be a fountain of knowledge about the history of our little house, so we decided to ask for his help in locating the exact position of our fosse. He wandered across our garden, his walking stick in one hand and a large iron sheep's crook in the other, his traditional blue cap pushed to the back of his head. "What on earth is he going to do with that? Divining?"

Arriving at the small raised flower bed on the edge of our patio, he tapped the ground. "C'est par ici" ('It's about here'), he confirmed. He then proceeded to drive the tip into the bindweed-covered soil some four or five times. Eventually we heard it strike something solid. "Eh voilà" he exclaimed, and instructed us to start digging. In just a few minutes of shovelling we had uncovered a large circular plastic lid. Gaston told us to remove it, a moment we had been not been relishing.

He explained that ours was only a small tank, possibly 1000 litres. All of the waste solids and liquids from the toilet and all the grey water waste from the sinks and bathroom flowed into this tank. The solids sank to the bottom and the liquids filled the rest of the space until they reached the outlet pipe. They then ran into forty metres of slotted pipes, the "soak-away", which zigzagged down the allotment. As it passed over the slots, the waste liquid soaked the ground, thereby providing valuable nutrients to the fruit and vegetables growing above.

We removed the lid. The smell that hit us still remains in our memory even today. "On English television programmes like "A Place in the Sun" about 'living the dream' in foreign climes, no one ever mentions such exotic moments as this" we moaned, quickly clamping down the lid.

Now, four years on, we knew that the smell from the "funny grey liquid" could only be coming from one thing, our septic tank. Once smelt, never forgotten! So when we got home from Bellegarde, we changed into our scruffiest gardening clothes and our muddy wellies. Spades in hand, we headed down to the "oozing" garden plot. We thrust the first spade into the ground, and, without warning, it sank down nearly a foot, releasing a torrent of grey gunge that gushed out like a fountain.

"Oh là là," or should that be "pooh là là?" Chris quipped, leaping back with an amazing burst of speed. We watched the stream flood down the garden and realised, just like the crew of Apollo 13, "We have a problem".

It is at moments like this, feeling somewhat overwhelmed (and squidgy underfoot!) that you realise you haven't a clue what to do. It was therefore reassuring that our two delightful neighbours, Yvette and Marcel, popped their heads over the garden wall. Marcel took in the problem immediately and told us "Dites donc, mes amis! That shouldn't be happening".
"We gathered that, but what do we do?" we asked.
"You'll have to dig out the hole and find the outlet pipe, which is probably fractured" he replied. We noticed a hint of a smile flickering across his face.
"Dig out !" we said, "that means digging through all this ooze".
With a Gallic shrug of the shoulders he replied, "Exactement! Bon courage, les voisins!".

Minutes later, having donned face masks to try to keep out the smell, we started playing "hunt the end of the pipe". It reminded us of digging holes on the beach when we were little. Every time we took a spade of earth and waste-matter out of the ground, the hole refilled. It took nearly half an hour to finally reach the offending pipe and that's when we made the shocking discovery. The pipe we uncovered was a "bog-standard" (no pun intended!) orange plastic drainpipe. No drainage slots, therefore no soak-away. This explained why the lake had built up at its exit.

A deep sense of foreboding overtook us. Over the next two hours we dug down around the pipe slowly moving up towards the septic tank. At times we were like builders, hacking away with a pickaxe to get through the hard clay. At other times we had to get down on our hands and knees like archaeologists, to excavate the soil with trowels in case we damaged the pipe.

When we were a couple of feet from the inspection chamber our hearts sank. We came to a piece of ground that was difficult to excavate, full of boulders and small stones. When we removed them, we uncovered the junction of the old slatted pipe that had led to an entire drainage system underneath our bottom garden. It had been totally cut off. It was no longer working. To quote from the famous Monty Python parrot sketch "It was deceased".

We needed help and needed it fast. We grabbed our French "Pages Jaunes" and started ringing round local drainage firms. They listened patiently as we outlined our predicament, but we were greeted every time with "Desolé, Madame…..", "Je regrette, Monsieur…" Every single company was "très pris". "Perhaps by September, Madame ….?" We were rapidly coming to the conclusion there must have been some virulent epidemic of "septic tank-itis" in the Creuse!

Then there arrives that sudden Einstein moment of realisation when you know, without a shadow of doubt, that life can be "crap" and for us this was literally the case. This was not a job that could be left until September. It had to be done now. We had no choice but to do it ourselves.

We rang an English friend, based in Normandy, who was registered as a drainage and septic tank engineer and he was really helpful. He gave us a potted "Install your own Soak-away Guide for Dummies" over the phone, pointing out that it could only be a stop-gap measure until, hopefully, the Government's programme of mains- drains installation would reach our hamlet. We made sure we took copious notes. The master plan, compiled by "the dummies", was formulated that evening over several compensatory glasses of Merlot. Anaesthetised by the wine, by the time we went to bed the task didn't seem quite so daunting.

The next morning, slightly fuzzy-headed, but more compos-mentis, we found that the challenge had grown to epic proportions. We had to dig out forty metres of trench, sixty centimetres deep. We had to tip four tons of gravel along the base of the trench on which to lay the slatted pipes. We had to remove four tons of displaced clay and earth and take it to the local "déchetterie". Then we had to lay the pipe-work along the gravel, and glue the sections together and top it all with more gravel. This would then be covered with a fabric called "geotextile", which allowed the rain to permeate the earth but would stop the soil getting into the pipes and blocking them. Finally we would have to spread a deep layer of topsoil over the entire length of the trench. We took a wild guess that we could manage about four metres each day, thus needing ten continuous days to complete the job.

The first morning, armed with spades and pickaxes, and bold in spirit, we were like the seven dwarves with a "Hi-ho, hi-ho it's off to work we go". By the last day it was an entirely different song, "Oh no, Oh no, to bloody work we go!". This was hard back-breaking slog, often undertaken in the intense heat of the afternoon. Looking back, there were, however, some treasured memories that still linger with us today.

We had to make numerous trips to our local builders' merchants to obtain the gravel, using our small trailer. In the yard at the depot we never ceased to be amazed at the strength and vigour of the owner. Although he was well into his eighties he was still working every day. After he had booked us in, he would cycle down to the gravel heap, get into the JCB and load our trailer. As soon as he finished dealing with us, and giving us a chitty for the bill, he would pedal off to some other part of the large site to serve his next customer. Tough as old boots, some of these locals were!

Every stage of the process was a steep learning curve. A trailer-full of 500 kilos of gravel is not an object to be taken lightly. In fact you quickly find it's not an object to be taken anywhere at all. When we reached home, we unhooked the trailer from the car. There it remained, unmoving, not a solitary inch. It was too heavy! Solution: -shovel some of the gravel into our wheelbarrow and take it down to the trench, one load at a time. After eight or nine arm-aching barrow loads, we found that we could just manage to manoeuvre the trailer into our top garden.

Pause for thought: - "A heavy trailer and a garden that slopes downhill". Thought: - "trailer will roll away". Thank goodness for the pile of good old French oak joists that happened to be lying around in the garden. We built a crash barrier with them, pulled the trailer through the gate and, as anticipated, it immediately began to gather momentum. But, it came to an abrupt halt as it hit the joist barrier. Immense relief, and only seven more loads to collect!

About halfway through the work, on a very hot afternoon we had really had enough! We downed tools and went up to the town to treat ourselves to a cream tea in the English tea-shop. As he came over to serve us, the owner remarked, "You two look whacked!" Hearing of our plight, he volunteered to help us the next day when the café would be shut. Sure enough, bright and early, he came on site and started attacking the next section of the trench. He worked tirelessly all day, and, as he finished, said he had really enjoyed it. Too much sun, obviously! But we never forgot this act of kindness.

Incredibly, on the tenth day, as hoped, we did finish the work. Except....

At the end of the run of pipe we had to dig out a large hole to make a stone pit. This would act as a final dispersal point if any liquid ran the entire forty metres down the drainage pipes. There was a great sense of achievement when we finished digging the square hole which was about a metre deep. We were just about to celebrate, when our friend, Guy, a man of few words, called round and headed down to us. We knew something was wrong as he shook his head.
"Not deep enough!"
"What?!!" How deep, then?"
"Let's say about two metres"
"Two metres! That's a bloody deep hole!"
"That's what's needed".

So we carried on digging....and digging. The pit was massive. Then we realised that no matter how much we searched the garden, we didn't have enough stones to fill it.
Solution? Obvious: - ask friends and neighbours.

What a response! Over the next few days they turned up with barrow after barrow- load of stones. In the end, there were so many that not only did we fill the stone-pit, but we had enough left over to be able to construct a new rustic stone wall at the bottom of the veggie patch.

Then came that wonderful morning when a local artisan finally connected our system to the fosse. "Turn on all the taps," he shouted, "and flush the loo!" As the water came cascading through, he peered down the inspection chamber. The liquid reached the new pipework and started to flow down the soak-away. It worked. It really worked. In fact, it worked so well that no liquid ever even reached the stone pit.

However, just a few weeks later, we discovered that we had new tenants living on top of our pile of stones, underneath the metal lid that was now covering it, tenants that we had no choice but to evict. As the chamber had become very damp and dank, over 200 slugs had moved in!

Our feelings about this mammoth undertaking can best be summed up by the title "The agony and the ecstasy". Our sense of achievement when the result of our labours had worked to perfection was the ecstasy. The "agony" was knowing that this could only be a short-term measure. We were already aware from our neighbours that there was soon to be an inspection of the septic tank and drainage systems of every property that was not already on mains drainage. We also knew that our system, being too small, too close to the house and to our neighbour's boundary, would fail any inspection. We would either be required to install an entirely new tank and dispersal system at a cost of several thousand euros or, best case scenario, our hamlet would be connected to a new mains drains system.

Solidarity was the keyword. All our neighbours, French and English knew that their septic tanks would not comply with the new standards. Many were living on their pensions and would never have been able to afford the cost of installing a new system. Soon the dreaded letters plopped into our mailboxes, notifying us of the official inspection, and, to add insult to injury, a cost of 56 euros per household for the privilege! So in true French fashion we protested. There is nothing more terrifying to local officialdom than residents protesting.

A petition was immediately drawn up, firmly but politely declining the inspection; -"They shall not pass!" The petitioners made clear their determination that no inspector would set foot on their property until serious consideration was given to connecting the whole hamlet to mains drains.

We all signed, and awaited the consequences. The "peasants" truly were revolting. The official inspections did not take place. The inspector had sent a copy of our petition to our local Mayor. For a while, all went very quiet. There was no word from the Town Hall.

However, several months later, a band of surveyors mysteriously descended on our hamlet. They conveyed the news that we were to be connected to mains drains! Victory announcements spread like wildfire, giving rise, in two instances, to wild dancing in the street, much communal kissing, self-congratulatory back-slapping, not to mention the cracking of numerous bottles of "vin rouge". I think we could, in all honesty, say we were "flushed with pride!"

"Vive La Révolution!"

Happiness is a wardrobe slowly rising in the air!

Six months on, our pipe burying exploits were now a far distant memory. It happened in the main street which ran through the centre of Bénévent L'Abbaye. We fell in love with this region, which is known for its vibrant green landscape, sustained by the combination of the summer heat and the sudden storms which can hit without warning. The locals say of this part of the Limousin that "you don't tan here, you rust".

Earlier that particular morning we had collected our petits pains from the artisan boulanger, savouring again the smell of the freshly baked breads and baguettes. Apart from an ancient Citroën Diane, the local road was virtually empty.

Now, just four hours later, during the lunchtime siesta, we were driving to the centre of the village on the way to see friends. Just before the bend that turned onto the main street we came to a grinding halt. Gridlock!

After a couple of minutes it was evident we were not going to budge. We got out of the car and walked around the corner fearing there might have been an accident.

As we reached the junction we could see immediately that the single road through the centre was blocked in both directions by a parked tractor. At its rear was a rusting farm trailer containing a motley assortment of household furniture.

A local farmer, in his blue overalls was standing in the centre of the tractor bucket. He was using both hands to hold a chest of drawers. He shouted to the tractor driver "Hup-là", and the bucket began to rise. It ascended to the first-floor window of a flat above the épicerie. Four arms appeared from behind the shutters and pulled the chest of drawers into the room.

The bucket was lowered, ready for its next piece of furniture. This time we saw a long glass oval mirror on a mahogany stand being placed in the bucket. The farmer clutched it carefully as once again it was raised to the window. The arms took it in.

This was our second year in France and we had come to deeply value the slower pace of life, the friendliness of wonderful neighbours and enjoying so many new tastes and experiences. We loved the vitality of the summer months with local villages holding their street brocantes and fêtes, complete with their parades of marching bands. The evenings would culminate in all types of music, dancing and spectacular firework displays

What amazed us, as we watched the tractor, was that all the car drivers and their passengers were out in the street, relaxed, laughing, absorbed in the whole event. The local tabac was doing a brisk trade as the spectators ordered their cafés, and installed themselves at pavement tables. They sheltered from the mid-day heat under the striped awnings. Others sat with them enjoying a pastis with its pungent aniseed aroma. Workmen, who had finished their twelve euro "Formule" meals, had come from the back room of the tabac to join everyone on the street. All eyes were fixed on the spectacle.

The bucket had been lowered again and this time a large traditional French wardrobe was lifted into it. It was so heavy that it took two willing bystanders to assist the farmer. It was obvious that it was not as secure as the other pieces due to its size. As the bucket began to rise, the wardrobe swayed precariously, caught by the lightest of breezes. The assembled crowd let out a concerned "Oh là là!" which reverberated around the street like a wave at a football match. As the wardrobe rose slowly in the air, silence descended. Everyone, ourselves included, held their breath. It rocked and swayed, and the young farmer was finding it difficult to keep it upright.

As it reached the window two ropes were quickly swung around it and the top was lowered slowly and carefully onto the sill. Then inch by inch it was pulled inside. The last thing we all saw were the wardrobe legs disappearing into the room.

Quite spontaneously a huge round of applause broke out, with shouts of "Encore!" and "Magnifique!" The young farmer in the bucket bowed to his audience, and they gave him another round of applause. He loved the adulation and took off his cap to salute them.

We were sharing with everyone a quite unique moment. As we stood there we felt that we had been fortunate to witness this rather unorthodox method of furniture removal. There was a sense of happiness and joy that was difficult to put into words.

Once the whole operation was finished, the tractor driver retracted the bucket into the safety of the tractor arm and backed into a tiny side street. The event was over, and everyone shook hands, bid each other farewell and went back to their cars to continue their journeys. The street was empty again.

As we drove off, we talked about what had happened, and we were conscious that there had been no blaring of horns, there had been no frustration or abusive language and no anger. It was a wonderfully unforgettable experience.

This event changed how we came to see our life in France. Until that afternoon, whenever we talked with family and friends, we still were referring to England as our home. From this time onwards, in our hearts and minds, we were no longer expats. We were bona fide French residents, totally at home in our hamlet on the edge of the town.

We would never have expected that such happiness and contentment could have come from a wardrobe slowly rising in the air.

It's a dog's life!

As any ex-pat knows, you are constantly seeking to find ways to meet new people and integrate into your community. Owning a dog, particularly a cute, lolloping, friendly mutt, is a sure-fire way of getting to know the neighbours.

We had been on holiday for four days in our French home and had been cooking on a tiny camping-cooker. We decided we needed a decent meal, so went to eat out at a nearby French restaurant in the little village of Chamborand.

There were five other families already seated as the waitress showed us to our table. As we sat down we made a delightful discovery. Three of the families had their dogs sitting beside their tables and we could see that this seemed the most natural thing in the world. It was our initiation into realising that the French are a nation of dog lovers. They take their pets to the many restaurants and cafés that welcome them. In the tabacs we often saw the patrons' beloved pooch snoozing in the bar, or doing the rounds of regulars. We would often be requested, "Please do not feed the dog any baguette or he'll become fat and lazy". We did think in some cases that these requests were coming rather too late. In the evenings, customers, with their dog in tow, would come in for a "Ricard", directing their pet over to a big bowl of water that the patron had provided.

One summer holiday, when Chris's son was visiting, we strolled into a popular bistro in Bourganeuf with our pet. The proprietor greeted us warmly and walked over to Ben who duly rolled over for a tummy tickle. A lady sitting at a nearby table also got up and stroked him saying "Qu'il est mignon!" (How cute he is).

Chris's son, Keith, said "What a difference from the UK. It's great you can bring the pooch along too. Just imagine what the 'Elf 'N Safety' brigade in England would say. They'd blow a gasket, shouting the odds at how many regulations were being contravened".

When we tootled up to the local bakery every morning to collect a freshly baked baguette, local villagers would come over to shake hands, "Bonjour Monsieur 'Dame" and stroke the dog, "Bonjour mon toutou". "Toutou" was an open invitation to strike up a conversation;" What a gentle face he has!" "What is his name?" "How old is he?" "Do you live round here?" "For how long?" "Do you like living in France?" etcetera, etcetera. We were also often praised for our assiduous use of pooh-bags, a practice that has unfortunately not yet extended to most other local dog-owning inhabitants!

When we had decided to move permanently to France, amid all the organisational tasks and bureaucracy, we had to factor in "Moving to France with a dog". At this time we had a four-year-old collie-cross, Ben.

First task: make an appointment with the vet for the required injections. We had done our research. We knew Ben would need his own "Pet Passport" in order to leave the country. The series of visits began.

We well remember one never-to-be-forgotten session in the vet's surgery. Ben was now due to have his rabies blood test. If all went well, in six months' time, this would allow him to acquire the necessary documentation so that he could travel to and from France.

"This won't hurt", the vet explained, "I'm just going to put some liquid on his paw to freeze his skin before taking some blood". Within seconds of it being applied, Ben shot off the table, climbed up Chris's chest and clamped his paws over her shoulder. He then let out a howl so long and piercing that it reminded us of the noise of a banshee in horror films. With that he collapsed onto her, shaking all over. As we emerged from the surgery with the quivering hound, all those in the waiting-room stared at us with fear and trepidation, wondering what on earth had caused this trauma. They were no doubt now dreading their own approaching foray into the torture chamber.

In due course, however, we did receive the passport, and we and our treasured pet became French residents in September 2006.

Arriving in the small hamlet, Ben jumped out of the car and lost no time at all in getting to know the local populace. In fine weather, everyone in our little lane left their front doors open, and Ben soon got into the habit of doing the rounds of the neighbours. They greeted him affectionately, and not infrequently with tasty titbits.

Some days, noticing he was missing, we would call "B-E-N".
"Il est chez moi, Christine, pas de problème!" would echo back. And there he would stay, lapping up the attention of a doting neighbour, until he decided it was time to move on to his next port of call.

Like all his French compatriots, he soon became expert at stretching out beside our table in a local bar when we met up with friends for aperitifs or curling up under the table while we ate a gargantuan 10 euro "formule" meal at lunchtime. He was no doubt hoping some local delicacy would accidentally find its way onto the floor without him having to move significantly to reach it!

On one occasion we went to have lunch on the terrasse of a particularly nice restaurant in a small, flower-decked square in Guéret, one of our nearest towns. We had attached Ben's lead to the table leg so that we could enjoy a leisurely meal in the warm sunshine. He took up his usual place under the table. As the coffee arrived, Chris glanced down, thinking how well-behaved he had been for what was now some considerable time. The lead was still tied to the table at one end and clipped to the dog's collar at the other, but the collar was unfortunately no longer attached to the dog!

"Nom d'un chien!" Total panic! We whistled, called his name, hunted round all the tables inside and outside. We asked other clients if they had seen him but to no avail. We quickly paid the bill and started searching, first the other cafes and eating places in the square, then the surrounding streets. Eventually, heading up a narrow alley, shaded from the midday sun, we spotted Ben, and realised he was not alone. He was fostering Anglo-French canine entente-cordiale with a rather stunning miniature poodle. We cornered our errant pooch, slipped the collar over his head and put a swift end to his dalliance with Fifi. He looked suitably indignant as we marched him away.

For Ben, this really was a dog's life!
However, as animal lovers, there was one aspect of life in rural France that we found difficult to come to terms with. Hunting, shooting and fishing were very popular in our region and, during the hunting season, two days a week and any Bank Holiday were designated for "La Chasse". Some local huntsmen kept their own hunting dogs in ramshackle sheds with small wire-netting runs, feeding them only on low-grade biscuits and exercising them only on hunt days. Once their working life was over, many of them ended up at the local SPA (Société Protectrice des Animaux) dogs' home. This was in stark contrast to the love and care lavished on pet dogs in France.

A few months after relocating to France we decided to make our first trip back to England to see family and friends. Ben was with us on board the cross-channel ferry sailing from Calais to Dover, one of the stormiest and roughest crossings we ever made. The pitch-and-toss of the vessel, riding the surging waves, left us both feeling very sick. We found it very hard to stay upright when attempting to walk about on board, and there was not the slightest chance of stretching our legs on the passenger deck. We were worried sick (literally) about Ben, who was three decks down below in the hatchback of our car. We were convinced he would be terrified as the boat pitched and rolled. Our concerns were not helped by a bright spark in the passenger lounge who announced, "I've been doing this trip every two months for the last seven years, and this is the worst I have ever known it! I'm surprised they even sailed today. I feel as sick as a dog!"

Oh dear! Our thoughts turned again to our poor pooch, no doubt suffering from "la nausée", with no one to comfort him, in car deck seven. In hindsight, we regretted giving him that big bowl of "Friskies" before boarding the ferry, picturing the inevitable outcome, and envisaging having a major clean-up job on our hands on disembarking at Dover.

Eventually, as the ferry approached the dock, we were allowed to access the car decks and we rushed back, green around the gills, to the vehicle. And there he was, curled up on his bed, sleeping like a baby, not a care in the world! So much for our concern!

In time, Ben took long-distance travelling in his stride, and we also became quite blasé about the procedures required to travel to and from the Continent with our pet. We discovered during our travels that there are numerous pet-friendly hotels, B&Bs and gîtes to be found.

On one visit to the U.K. we were passing through Passport Control and had scanned Ben's microchip as requested, but we were asked to get him out of the car. "Oh no! What has gone wrong? Have we forgotten some vital operation? Perhaps the vet's treatment the previous day has not been recorded correctly in his passport." But it turned out that the girl in the booth simply liked the look of Ben's photo, and felt like giving him a big fuss.

Ben adored his walks in France, especially on a footpath that led from our home up to Bénévent L'Abbaye. He could run, explore, chase rabbits, sniff scents on wild animals that had passed that way in the night, and burrow through the dense undergrowth. Despite his monthly tick and flea treatment, we regularly had to remove ticks from his coat when we reached home.

It was during one of these daily walks, when he was only six years old, and, as far as we knew, a perfectly fit and healthy dog, that his legs suddenly buckled under him and he collapsed. We had to carry him back home and immediately lifted him into the car and took him to the local vet's surgery. With great sympathy our vet diagnosed an incurable heart problem.

"I'm sorry, but there is nothing I can do. He could last another two weeks, but he would be unable to walk", the vet said very quietly. We therefore had to take the devastating decision to have our treasured pet put to sleep. The shock was even greater because there had been no warning signs, so we were totally unprepared for this sad outcome.

"Never again. No more dogs we vowed, grief-stricken at losing such a cherished companion. Even our two neighbours Yvette and Solange were in tears when we told them the news.
The very next day, "toc, toc", "Coucou!".Yvette tapped the door and came in. "Un petit cadeau" she said, handing over a cuddly toy that bore more than a passing resemblance to Ben to "fill the gap left by your lovely dog".

We placed the toy on the rug by the wood-burner, Ben's favourite spot in the house, and thought how lucky we were to have such caring and considerate neighbours.

Yet, six weeks later, there we were, on our way to a remote sheep-farm near Lake Vassivière to meet Kakou, a three-month-old pure border collie bundle of fluff. We fell in love with him as soon as we saw him, and he came charging over to us, eager for a fuss. The farmer's wife assured us that he would make a great family pet, even though he came from sheepdog parents. One of his grandparents had, in fact, been a French champion.

Kakou was totally adorable even though he was a rogue. He had boundless, unremitting energy. He would play and play and play. By the end of the day we would be shattered trying to keep up with him while he would be as fresh as a daisy. Just watching him charging in and out of the patio doors and round and round the garden was exhausting!

He had the frustrating ability to chew anything in sight. When Martin and Susan, two of our close friends, came round, ostensibly to see us and chat over coffee and cake, but more likely to make acquaintance with our new puppy, they asked, "What is Kakou doing with that piece of wood in his mouth?"

We were the proud owners of a small and very beautiful little French side table, which up till then had had two spindles between the base of the legs. Now it only had one, as Kakou charged out onto the patio proudly brandishing the other in his mouth.

In anticipation of his arrival, we had fenced our top garden to make a secure area for him to play in, the fencing being attached to posts which we fixed behind concrete slabs. The little devil continually made us laugh trying to dig a hole in the concrete to get under the fence. Turn your back for one minute and our little escapologist would discover a new way to explore pastures new. The one-metre-high patio fencing was no obstacle to our curious puppy, and the gate to our vegetable garden merely another physical challenge.

"Toc, toc. Peter! Christine! Have you lost anything?"

It was Solange, clutching our mischievous pet who had found his way into her back garden while she was hoeing the weeds. "He's a scamp, but cute with it!"

Cute he might have been, but this pup was clearly a free spirit, with a mission to roam. In desperation we purchased a doggy-exercise device consisting of a metal stake anchored in the lawn, and a long chain attached to his collar. This allowed our tethered puppy to run round and round in safety without doing his Houdini act and disappearing among the cabbages. We ensured that the chain was just long enough to keep him on the grass, thereby preventing him from totally destroying the flower beds and rockery plants. He was soon spinning round the perimeter of our lawn like some whirling Dervish. At least this way we knew where he was, and could get on with the daily tasks and chores with the peace of mind that he was not halfway to Bénévent!

Although we walked him three or four times every day it was never enough for him. He would still be raring to go, whilst we collapsed, "ouf!", in an exhausted heap on the garden sunloungers. It soon became clear that Kakou needed far more exercise than we would ever be able to give him.

The crunch came when two of our friends, Mark and Sally, from nearby Vieilleville came over for a meal with us. "You two look shattered", Sally observed. And we realised we were. The combination of long walks, DIY, maintaining the large "potager" and the unseasonal heat were taking their toll. After three months and much soul-searching, we reached the reluctant decision that we could not keep Kakou. This dog, no matter how adorable and lovable, needed to be a working dog, not a family pet.

In a nearby town there was an excellent SPA animal rescue centre and we called there to explain the situation and to enquire if they knew of any farmer needing a sheepdog puppy.

"Yes," said the manager, "we have one farmer who has been on our waiting list for months. He's desperate to find a puppy to train to the sheep. His collie is nearing the end of its working life. Every time he has rung we have had to tell him that we have hunting dogs, but not a single sheepdog."

She rang Monsieur Giron while we were there. We could sense his excitement on the other end of the phone when he heard a puppy was now available. He arranged to come over to our house the very next morning at 10 a.m.

He arrived on the dot, his off-white, mud-bespattered Renault van rattling to a halt outside our door. Dressed in his "bleu de travail", and sporting a large flat cap to match, he shook our hands vigorously, smiling broadly. His weather-beaten face was a picture when he saw Kakou, who had bounded over to greet him. There seemed to be an instant bond between them. He immediately pronounced Kakou "perfect", beaming from ear to ear. He was certain he would make an excellent working sheepdog.

In preparation for his new arrival, he had already managed to purchase a collar and lead, and a bright-green dog bed covered in criss-cross patterns of tiny black paw-prints, which was in the back of his van. He said he lived alone on the farm, and assured us he would take good care of our puppy. He would be both a companion and a working dog, training alongside his present sheepdog who was on his last legs and really too old to work on the farm for much longer. He assured us Kakou would sleep in the kitchen, not in an outside barn as is customary with farm dogs. We chatted over a cup of coffee, while Monsieur Giron gently stroked the little dog who amazingly lay quietly by his feet. When he drove off with Kakou with profuse thanks and much hand-shaking, it was a moment of great heartbreak for us. Out came the paper hankies yet again!

Two weeks later the phone rang. It was Monsieur Giron. He informed us that he was delighted with Kakou who was already out on the farm with him every day and loving his new life. He said he was "impeccable".

After that he rang us regularly to provide progress reports, all confirming how intelligent his protégé was, how well he was doing and how quickly he was adapting to his new life. This confirmed our view that we had made the right decision in letting him go. However, we could not help but feel his departure acutely. "Never again! No more dogs!" we swore.

So how come, two months later, were we the proud owners of Beau, our Labrador-retriever cross? Well, he was the runt of a large litter that had been left behind by his English owner who could not find enough work locally to remain in France. Two English neighbours, John and Kate, had taken in the two last remaining puppies as a temporary favour, but, already having three dogs of their own, knew they needed to rehome them. One of our close friends, Jenny, went over to see the two puppies, and decided to take one of them.

"I'd have had them both if it was up to me," she sighed, "but Pete would have hit the roof! We've already got a menagerie; dogs (three now), cats, budgies and chickens. But the other one is GORGEOUS!"

Well, that did it. Here we go again! We reached for the phone.
"Come right over", Kate said.

As soon as we saw him, and he looked up at us with his big brown eyes we were smitten. "We'll have him" we said in unison, not even needing to discuss the matter first. And so Beau became our third dog in France.

Beau had a beautiful, gentle disposition, and a very loving nature that drew you to him immediately Once again, our neighbours were besotted with our new pet. Being part retriever, he had the endearing characteristic of presenting a soft toy to anyone who called at the house, be it the post lady or the boiler maintenance man. He even carted his favourite lion toy down the road on his daily visit to our neighbour Solange.

He had only been with us for three days when we had an "apéro" party at our home to celebrate the completion of work on an extension to our home. The house we had originally purchased as a holiday home had proved just too small as a permanent residence, so we had used part of the large top garden to extend, with the addition of a new "salon".

"So when is the topping-out ceremony?" our neighbour Marcel enquired, with more than a degree of self-interest, we thought.
"What topping-out ceremony?" we asked in panic.

"It's the local custom here. You invite everyone round to celebrate when new building work is completed, and throw a spray of flowers onto the roof to bring good luck to the household."

Upon further investigation, we discovered that friends, neighbours, family, local dignitaries and any artisans who have been involved in the construction process all usually receive an invitation. A perfect excuse for a knees-up! As it was the summer holidays, many of our friends and neighbours rolled up with their families.

The children, polite and well-behaved to a T spent the whole afternoon playing with Beau; throwing balls and sticks, chasing him round the garden, catching him, rolling over on the grass, and giving him endless fuss and cuddles. They only stopped briefly to graze, with true Gallic appreciation, on our extensive buffet, washing it all down with copious amounts of Sprite and Fanta.

As he was still somewhat of an unknown quantity, we felt we needed to keep a close eye on our new pet, but we need not have feared. He loved every minute of it. He was as gentle and patient with the children as he had been from the start with us. We knew instinctively that we could trust him completely.

The afternoon proved a great success. Many a canapé was consumed along with colourful mounds of crudités, "dips à la tomate et aux herbes fraîches", a selection of cheeses and charcuterie from all corners of France, and a mountain of wedges of "pain à l'ancienne", slathered in lashings of Normandy butter, all accompanied by a selection of wines on offer that week at "Champion".

Prompted by those present, and having refilled everyone's glasses yet again to drink a toast to the new extension, we lobbed our colourful Jardiland mixed bouquet onto the roof of the new "salon", to shouts of "Bravo!". There it remained for several weeks until the decaying blooms were washed away in a cloudburst during one of the many electric storms we experienced in the summer months. After all the eating, drinking and bonhomie, everyone departed to eat their proper evening meal. Well, some things in France are truly sacrosanct!

Beau settled in rapidly and it soon felt like he had always been part of the family. He had two great loves. The first was jumping into water at every opportunity which we knew came from daily walks by the river with his previous owner. The second was bathing or rolling in any mud patches he could find. He also had an uncanny knack of discovering hidden stagnant pools, usually covered with duckweed or foul-smelling green slime. This often meant we would have to hose him down in the garden when he returned from "walkies", looking like the monster from the deep.

He was the only dog we ever had who would sit out in the garden in a thunderstorm and watch the 14th of July Bastille Day firework display from the vantage point of the patio. However, this situation was sadly to change. When, on one occasion, we were walking him on a local public footpath and came across a group of huntsman garbed top-to-toe in matching, full green-and-brown flecked camouflage gear, in a copse beside the path. Suddenly they started firing furiously at some prey unfortunate enough to have wandered into range among the trees. Beau froze, then, emitting a loud howl, turned and ran. We retraced our tracks, and eventually discovered him back at the house, half an hour later. It took several weeks of walking him on the lead past that spot before he would run free there again, and, from that day onwards, he was terrified of loud noises, thunder, fireworks and gunfire.

Beau is a wonderful dog, so loving and caring. Whenever we are unwell he will come and lie down alongside us for hours. It was, therefore, a cause of great concern when, in early June 2010, at about one o'clock in the morning, we heard him howling as if in pain. Chris went downstairs, and he was pacing up and down the room, and sniffing by the front door.

"I'd better see if he needs to go out."
On opening the back door, he rushed out into the garden. Chris called him in, a few minutes later, and he seemed to settle down in his basket so she went back to bed. More howls and wandering round the room.

"He must be ill", Chris said, poking me in the ribs. "We'll need to take him to the vet's in the morning. I'd better sleep downstairs with him tonight."

Grabbing a spare duvet she went downstairs, and settled down on the klic-klac. Silence....then more whining and restlessness. Another howl, this time coming from the other side of the front door. Chris opened the window and metal shutters and peered out. There, lying pressed against the threshold of our cottage, was the farmer's Alsatian bitch, on heat, and seeking the company of a handsome mate!

"Va-t'en!", yelled Chris fiendishly, trying not to wake all the neighbours, waving her arms wildly in the Alsatian's direction. But the dog disregarded her totally. She simply stayed put all night, refusing to budge. And Beau continued to whine and sniff at the front door, all night!

At 7.00 a.m., having had no sleep at all, Chris had had enough. She rang Bernard, the farmer, and explained the whereabouts and shenanigans of his missing dog. He came down straight away and carted her off, promising to keep her shut up at night while she was "en chaleur". Beau, having suffered his disturbed night, spent most of the next day sleeping – "dog tired" you might say! Thereafter the Alsatian became known locally as "Beau's girlfriend".

Wherever we go with Beau, he is always greeted and patted by strangers who all say what a lovely, friendly face he has. All animal lovers are conscious of the deep bond of affection that exists between them and their pet, and dogs have long been seen as "man's best friend". Our three dogs have given us so much love, fun and laughter. They have been loyal and faithful companions, sharing with us the good times and bad. And they have all, in their own unique ways, enriched and enhanced our lives.

Whatever you do, don't let go of the rope!

We had left Ben at home throwing a real sulk. He'd retreated to his dog bed in disgust. We had gone to Limoges airport to collect our friends John and Maggie and their two children who were still excited following the flight.

"I know," Andrea shouted, "let's play I spy".

"Great idea" their mum replied, eager to keep them amused on the way back to the house. "You go first".

"I spy with my little eye something beginning with T" Andrea announced.

All of us shouted out in unison, "Trees".

"How did you guess?" she whinged. "You cheated!"

Not exactly a difficult challenge when there are 584,000 hectares of woods in the Creuse. Some of the trees are conifers, but most are deciduous, birch, oak, beech and chestnut.

Soon after we emigrated to France, we began to discover some of the husbandry traditions and woodcarving skills that determine so much of the life of the forests.

During one summer, a highly skilled wood carver brought a large section of an oak tree trunk into the village square, just before our "Moutonnades" Festival began. Using only a small chainsaw and a range of hand tools he carved out a magnificent wooden bench from the single piece of wood, inscribing the name of our town on the back of the seat. A group of local "retraités", enjoying the popular game of "pétanque" in the tree-lined close beside the Abbey, strolled over to watch.

"C'est impressionnant!" they exclaimed. And it was an incredibly impressive piece of craftsmanship. To our knowledge, this bench is still in the square and is constantly admired by the tourists and pilgrims who visit the famous ancient twelfth-century Abbey.

One afternoon we were on the way to visit a local beauty spot and commented on a particular hillside, resplendent with different species of trees clinging to its slopes. Just two weeks later, when we passed the same way again, it was totally denuded, leaving only a scarred brown landscape.

That evening, sitting in our local tabac, we were chatting with a retired French forestry worker.

"Why have all those trees been cut down?" we asked.

"The felling is essential" he explained, "to provide the timber for a wide variety of uses, but especially for fuel. The planting of the saplings, the growing of the trees and the harvesting of logs is a very well-planned process. It is carried out in close co-operation with the region's saw-mills. It's normally the case that, within a short time of felling, the ground will be cleared and new saplings planted. If this did not happen, in twenty or thirty years' time, there would be a shortage of wood".

A few months later, passing the area once again, we were amazed to see that the barren earth was covered in new foliage, now giving it a vibrant and fresh new appearance.

As time went by we were also to discover something heart-warming about the honesty and integrity of those who live and work in the countryside. We became increasingly aware of piles of felled timber that varied in size, from a couple of hundred logs to huge commercial stacks. These would be sited just off the main roads. in open areas, quite often alongside public footpaths and bridle paths.

No wood was ever stolen. Even though everyone had need of timber as fuel for log fires and wood-burners, it would only ever be removed and used by the owners.

Our lack of knowledge about tree propagation led to various humorous interludes with our local French friends. We had been invited for aperitifs to the home of a local farmer, Bernard, and his wife, Françoise, one wet September evening.

We remarked, "We've just finished stacking our logs for the winter today, but have not had a chance to cover them yet, so they will be soaked through by now. We've been told that wet wood won't burn".

A polite, barely disguised guffaw followed!

"So you're afraid all your wood will be too wet, then?" the farmer asked.

"Well, it's been pouring all day!" we replied.

A broad smile spread across his face.

"You do not understand 'wet wood', do you? It is 'wet' when it has recently been cut down, because the sap is still in the timber. This gave it its life whilst it was growing, but after the felling, the sap must have time to dry out. This normally takes about two years, which is why you see wood-piles dotted over the area. It's drying out, ready for use. The rain falling on it makes very little difference when you come to burn it."

We both felt a bit "wet behind the ears", somewhat embarrassed at our lack of knowledge of all things rural! But we shared gamely in the mirth and merriment at the apparent dumbness of "Les rosbifs". By the end of the evening, and several tumblers of eau de vie later, communicating in a bizarre combination of pidgin French and English, we were all screaming uproariously at the merest hint of a jest. The words "bois de chauffage" (firewood) and "la flotte" (the slang for "rain"), which strangely recurred more and more frequently as the evening progressed, provoked paroxysms of uncontrollable laughter. By the time we staggered home close to midnight, we hardly noticed the torrents of rain still sheeting down on our heads.

There were occasions when a ruthless cutting of the trees became necessary. There is a certain combination of heavy rainfall and long hours of sun that leads to the trees increasing in height very quickly. It is impossible to monitor every tree, and at times their growth threatens both power and telephone lines. Falling branches can interrupt the electric supply during high winds and snowy weather. It means that the utility companies have no choice but to chop straight through the trunks.

One January morning, after we had lost our power supply during the night, we heard the buzz of multi-chainsaws nearby. A team of men were working in the field adjacent to an empty property. Seeing what was happening, we asked nosily,

"Why are you cutting straight across the trunks of the trees, rather than lopping off the branches that are touching the wires?"

The foreman replied, "We cannot afford the cost in time and manpower to keep coming back again and again. We don't have the time to try to trace the owners of the patches of land like this, as many are no longer either known or resident in the department. The only way to ensure that the trees will not cause further damage is to cut them down completely".

"C'est triste", Chris replied, thinking about the effect on the environment.

"Je suis d'accord, Madame. Mais c'est nécessaire."

The tree tops will be left on the land where they have fallen if it is private land, and will only be removed if there is any threat to traffic or public safety. It was sad, as we walked the dog each day, to see the remaining decapitated stumps sticking up vertically across the landscape.

On English television and in the press, there is often criticism levelled at English people living in France who claim their winter fuel allowance. As I was thinking about this story, I had gone into Birmingham and was sitting in a café drinking my latte, when I overheard an indignant group of pensioners.

"It's a bloody disgrace! They can go off to all these hot countries and laze around in the sun all day, and then have the cheek to claim winter fuel allowance! What a nerve!"

Setting aside any political arguments about benefits, there is a major misunderstanding about winters in France and other parts of the Continent. From late October to the following March, we could have very cold weather, and the nights could often be very bitter. Minus fifteen degrees would not be unusual for us during January and February. Spend too long outside in those temperatures, and you'd end up looking like an Aldi frozen chicken. The net result was that we often had to keep the wood-burner going all through the night for the house to remain acceptably warm.

To achieve this, we had to have a good supply of dry logs. We valued the help and advice of our local sawmill, sited just on the edge of Bénévent. We would order our wood supply in the early summer for delivery during September. The "stères" of oak and beech would be dropped by truck in the street and we would then wheelbarrow them into the garden to stack in the wood store.

There was a correct and an incorrect way to stack logs. As we started to tackle our very first pile, we naturally chose the incorrect way. A neighbour, Henri, who lived on the edge of our hamlet, had stopped at the fence to watch the entertainment.

"Hang on a minute!" He shot through the gate, and, with our permission (very freely given) he proceeded to kick away all the base logs we had laid.

"It is important that you allow air to circulate up through the stack." He then demonstrated criss-crossing the logs in a neat, attractive, sort of herring-bone pattern, so that, as the pile ascended towards the heavens, it did not collapse, and still allowed air to pass between the layers.

Every time we had a wood delivery, we had to let our neighbours know, as our log- mountain blocked the road until we managed to stack it. A secondary reason for informing them was that it invariably resulted in the appearance of extra pairs of hands to expedite the work. It was most heart-warming to see a posse of wheelbarrows descending the lane each time a load was dropped. This may, of course, have had something to do with needing the use of the road before the month was out!

On one particular delivery, our sawmill made a mistake with the size of the logs they brought. We must stress that this only ever happened once. Our logs had to be cut at the mill into 33-centimetre lengths, as this was the maximum size that could fit easily into the wood-burner. The driver delivered our order, depositing a pile of 50-centimetre logs by the gate! We realised, as the logs hit the road, that they were all the wrong size, but by that time it was too late. The truck had been emptied.

Together with the driver and two neighbours we spent a very happy half hour lobbing them all back onto the truck. The driver was most embarrassed and apologetic, but everyone patted him on the back, at pains to bolster his confidence.

"Not to worry. It could happen to anyone. It's an easy mistake to make."

"It's never happened to me before," he said, quite dejected, "and what is the boss going to say?"

"How will he ever know? We certainly won't tell him" we reassured him.

"Merci beaucoup! I appreciate that" he replied, clambering into his cab and driving back up the road. When he returned later with the second load, and this time 33-centimetre logs, we noticed that the truck seemed unusually full, with a higher stack of logs on board than usual. The driver up-ended the load in the street, and, after getting our signature on the "facture", started the engine and left. We still remain convinced to this day that we caught a mischievous wink of the eye as he drove off, but there again, we could have been imagining it!

We were affected by changes in the weather in France just as we are here in England. The winter of 2009 was an extremely long one, lasting until early May. One consequence of this was that our local sawmill, along with many others across the region, had to meet unusually high demands for logs, draining their reserves. They had to break into the supply that was really meant for the next winter.

In the late summer of 2010 we went to the mill to order winter wood, only to be told they had no dry timber left. They would only be able to supply green, that is, wet, wood. We had no choice but to accept the situation, and in due course the delivery was made. We had to think through very carefully how we were going to cope with wet wood. Our solution was to empty our main room of some of our furniture and stack large piles of logs inside so that we could at least begin to dry them before use. The living room looked like a wood-yard, with logs, shavings and woodlice everywhere.

This made us realise that events like this were taken in their stride by older French residents. Many rarely decorated their homes. They had much more sensible priorities, like preparing gastronomic delights at every meal, and spending abundant amounts of quality time with the family. They were certainly not into shunting the furniture around on a weekly basis, and attempting to achieve the gold-star "Homes and Gardens" level of decorative perfection that we English insisted on aspiring to. They could easily live with a stack of wood in the salon if that was what was needed. Only our English friends made witty quips:

"Going into the forestry business, are we?" "Are you registered for this?" "Can we put our order in for next year?" etcetera, etcetera.

There was one further piece of useful information that came from a young French friend, and this was to do with the lighting of a reluctant wood-burner. It would appear to be a simple enough task. Clean out the old ashes, place the kindling sticks and firelighters on the metal base, and light. However it was never quite that easy. Some days we would have a blazing fire within minutes, and others we could struggle for over an hour to get the thing going.

During our time in Bénévent, there were many occasions when someone would organise informal meetings between English and French locals to practise our mutual conversation. Many French people wanted to improve their English, just as we constantly tried to improve our French.

At one of these meetings, I was talking to François, a young car mechanic, about our fire-lighting problem.

He gave me a knowing look and said "You have a problem with the wind".

I went very red-faced, not sure I had heard him correctly. There was no need to be personal!

Seeing my reaction he said again "You have a problem with the wind. It all depends how it blows round your chimney".

"Ouf!" I breathed a sigh of relief.

He continued, "There is nothing you can do about it. Some days it will be good and some days it will be bad".

Apparently, the atmospheric conditions affect how your fire burns. Some days it makes you want to swear, because the damn thing just won't go!

There is something very special each November when everyone has to light their fires again. We loved to stroll up the road, which climbed steeply behind our garage, until we were above the level of all the roofs in our hamlet. Each chimney would be sending out ribbons of smoke, the distinctive smell of burning logs lingering in the cool, crisp air, evoking the cosiness and comfort inside.

We were always impressed by the dexterity and skill of the woodcutters, and the casual ease with which they handled their chainsaws. They were able so nimbly to move among branches without, apparently, the slightest fear.

Now, we knew that we were not woodcutters, but there was one particular occasion when we faced the challenge of cutting down a tree.

In the winter of 2007 we had a two-week period of torrential rain. As this water cascaded down our garden, the pressure it generated proved too much for our boundary retaining wall at the bottom of the garden. Part of it collapsed.

We decided this was a job for a professional, and put the work out to tender. The fallen section of wall was rebuilt in the early summer of 2008 by a local builder/stonemason. Superb job! Wonderful! Wall-work complete! Well, not quite.

As we settled his "facture" our friendly artisan gave us the bad news. The other end of the wall at the bottom of our garden was bulging out as tree roots were putting it under strain.

"What's the solution?" we asked.

"Cut down the tree" he replied. "I know someone who can do it for you, if that would help".

"Don't worry," we responded, "we can cut it down ourselves". He looked genuinely surprised, and somewhat sceptical, and, as he departed, asked us to give him a ring if we decided we needed a real tree-surgeon.

First of all we thought it prudent to check with our local Mairie that our tree was not subject to a Protection Order. Fortunately, there being no such order, we were free to cut it down.

The work presented us with three problems:

Firstly, all along the wall below the tree there was a three-strand electrified fence. This ran all round the edge of the local farmer's fields to ensure that his cattle could not escape. We could not risk branches falling on the wires and cutting the power.

Secondly, growing all around the base of the tree was a boxwood bush, a "buis" a beautiful green colour, and used every Easter in the Abbey as part of their ceremonials. As it apparently has deep significance for the worshippers, Yvette asked if we could take great care not to damage it because there were very few of these bushes left in the area.

Finally — a not insignificant consideration — our trusty stonemason had informed us that our boundary wall was full of snakes, "vipères", all through the summer, and it would be better if they were not disturbed, a sentiment with which we wholeheartedly agreed.

The day of the felling duly arrived. We assembled all the kit we needed: gloves; goggles; chainsaw; handsaw; protective helmets; rope and a very comprehensive first aid kit, just in case.

The tree was about five metres tall and we had mapped out an action plan of how we were going to cut it down.

As the chainsaw kicked into life, Marcel, watching from the safe distance of his patio, called out, "Bon Courage, Les Anglais!" Unbeknown to us, every step of the operation was to be observed by Solange, sitting beside her phone in case she needed to dial "les pompiers" in a permanent state of, she told us later, "fear and trepidation".

I began by lopping the lower branches that were growing out over the bottom wall. For this procedure, I was working at a height of about three metres, precariously wedged in the fork of the tree. It was important that these were cut first to stop the trunk of the tree, with me in it, simply toppling over the wall. This would most certainly have destroyed the electric fencing, not to mention my credibility and confidence.

Each branch was roped prior to the cutting, and, as it began to fall, Chris's job was to haul it into the garden, ensuring that it missed the "buis". All well and good, but progress was painfully (literally) slow. We proceeded, branch by branch, hoping we were not bothering our resident snakes too much, until we came to the greatest challenge – a very large branch, some four metres in length, which stretched right out over the field.

"This one's going to be difficult" I said, "It's the longest and the heaviest by far". I was perched in the tree as Chris asked annoyingly, "So how are we going to get the rope on it?"

There was a pause for reflection (and possibly quick prayer at the time) before I came up with the solution – "There's only one way. I'll have to drag myself along the branch as far as it's safe to go". With that piece of bravado, and sitting with legs astride, I inched myself slowly forward, clinging on for dear life.

It was while I was sitting suspended over a ten-foot drop, and looking down into the piles of fresh cow dung below, that I wondered if I should have taken up the builder's offer of a trained professional he knew to do the job. Chris threw the rope out and I tied it securely around the branch. I then edged my way backwards, even more slowly, until I reached the safety of the trunk. Chris took up the tension. We had reached the point of no return.

"Whatever you do, don't let go of the rope!" I shouted.

The chainsaw did its work and cut through the branch, near to the central trunk. There was a tremendous "crack!" as it broke, and Chris pulled with all her might as I ducked out of the way. Incredibly, the giant limb landed on the garden.

"Bravo!" yelled Marcel, breaking into a round of applause.

At this moment our "watcher", Solange, came scurrying across the garden.

"Mon Dieu Peter! What are you doing, climbing about in trees at your age?" she exclaimed. "And Christine, I was expecting to see you go catapulting over the wall at any moment! J'étais sur les nerfs!" And she was not the only one!

The work was done for the day. We crawled back to the house, with a mixture of exhaustion and exultation at what we had achieved.

The only remaining task was to destroy the remaining trunk of the tree, ensuring then that the roots could cause no further damage.

We visited our local Bricomarché DIY store, and were sold a tin of powder that would, we were assured, deal with the stump. When we got home we read the instructions:

On the top of the flat area of the stump drill ten or twelve large bore holes and place a small amount of the powder at the bottom of each hole.

So far, so good

Then fill each hole with petrol, and, standing well back, set them all on fire.

The tin said the fire would then burn for at least a day as the remains of the stump were consumed.

Set light to the petrol? Not bloody likely! I had visions of the ensuing fire not only consuming the stump but also the "buis", the snakes, the electric fence, and anything else that got in the way. The box was consigned safely to the garage shelf, never to see the light of day again.

Over the next few months I worked with great patience, slowly but surely with a rip saw to cut away at the base, and eventually succeeded in stopping it growing new shoots. We cut up the timber and stowed it away in our wood store. It gave us great satisfaction to burn our "home grown" logs.

In the Creuse, even the trees have stories to share.

"Henri, porte la table!"

Finishing off the tree trunk required one kind of patience which was easy to accept.

However, one summer lunchtime our patience was severely tested.

"I'm sorry but you'll have to wait five hours."

No, we were not visiting the local hospital A&E here in England. We were at a brocante held in our little town of Bénévent during the Moutonnades Festival, held at the end of August. The steward was very insistent.

Our Fête, which celebrated the different varieties of sheep raised in the Limousin, began on a Friday evening with music and dancing in the village square and lasted until Sunday evening.

We could still remember one "earth-shattering" experience that first year at the house. The Saturday morning began with an awful shock. Fast asleep in bed, we were woken at the crack of dawn by the sound of what we thought was a huge explosion.

"What the hell was that?" Peter shouted in panic, fearing our gas cooker had blown up. As we scrambled downstairs there was another almighty bang.

We ran out into the garden but our gas tank and house seemed to be all perfectly fine. Then, looking up the valley, we saw crowds of people gathered outside the back of the Abbey, standing around an ancient cannon that was announcing the start of the day's celebrations.

It was two years later that we decided to try to sell some unwanted items at the Saturday brocante. French brocantes, popular in many towns and villages, are like car-boot sales, but not quite. They are held in the main streets, and many householders book the pavement space outside their front door so they can bring out and take in goods on their stalls throughout the day.

We duly arrived on site at 6.00 a.m. with our car and trailer loaded with things to sell, and we were very lucky to be allocated a street corner pitch in the very heart of the town.

For anyone who has never visited a French brocante, it is a truly memorable experience. The stalls are set out with a rich variety of goods, ranging from beautiful objets d'art to rusty old pieces of metal. In tact there are lots of shabby, broken-to-bits items on display, but even these are carefully scrutinised by the many potential buyers.

There are usually also stalls selling rustic furniture in various states of disrepair ("distressed" isn't the word – these are often downright woebegone), eagerly sought out by English, Dutch and Parisian visitors and traders. We noticed over the years that the prices of old French furniture rose considerably. We asked a French trader why this was happening and he explained, "It is all the English who want it, not the French. We do not want this type of thing in our homes any more. But there are plenty of keen foreign buyers, so we have naturally raised our prices. It's a question of supply and demand".

The items on display on our stall stood out because nearly everything we had to sell was modern. Just as in England, we were pounced on by early-birds looking for the juicy worm. It was like a feeding frenzy!

"Ten euros for the lot" we said, replying to a question about the price of a box of assorted tools.

"I'll give you five if I can take them now" our would-be buyer offered. The haggling had begun. We eventually shook hands at eight euros with both parties feeling that honour had been satisfied.

It was a boiling hot day and on our corner we had very little shade. We were delighted, therefore, to find that by 1.00 p.m., virtually everything had gone, leaving only a few distinctly tatty items remaining.

"Well, that's it," we said "the rest can go to the tip! Time to pack up and go home".

Only, it wasn't.

No one had told us that stallholders could not leave until 6.00 p.m. We eventually tracked down a street-marshal and asked, in our most polite, obsequious French if he could please slightly move the exit barrier, which was just up the road from us, for "un petit moment", as we had sold out.

"Impossible" he retorted. "No one can leave for another five hours."

"Wh….a…a….t?!" Five more hours in the blazing sun, with only a few bits of junk left.

So stay we did, achieving the sale of about one item every hour. In the closing minutes, we spotted a lively group of young bucks, slightly the worse for wear, heading towards us on the way to the exit.

"Dix centimes, la pièce" we hollered, "offers accepted!"

They descended on our stall like a plague of locusts, and snapped up every last thing, departing in high spirits, clearly thinking they had got a bargain. And we were relieved that nothing was left, with no trip to the tip needed.

We finally got home about 6.45 p.m. We had invited friends round for a barbecue, so immediately began the preparations, and they duly arrived about 7.30 p.m. This was always one of our favourite moments as we sat out in the garden on a balmy summer's evening after a delicious barbecue, sharing a bottle of rosé and watching the sun go down.

At 10 p.m., with our glasses refilled, our eyes turned towards the Abbey.

Suddenly the sky was illuminated by a truly magnificent display of fireworks and we were in the ideal spot to watch it. It lasted for a good twenty minutes with spectacular rockets igniting the whole of the horizon. Marcel and Yvette had their family round and were also sitting out on their patio.

As the fireworks ended, Yvette came to the wall.

"Bonsoir, les voisins. C'était magnifique, n'est-ce pas?"

"Oui, formidable!" we responded.

Then with a slightly different tone to her voice she said mischievously "There goes half our year's rates up in smoke!"

We all burst out laughing.

The Sunday morning was given over to craftsmen and women selling their wares in one part of the town, with pens of sheep and lambs filling another of the streets. The bars would be overflowing and the little square marquees selling beers and pastis would be thronging with customers, sitting on wooden benches or standing around in groups, laughing and joking. The atmosphere was relaxed, informal and convivial.

We enjoyed visiting brocantes in other areas which were often linked to local "Foires", where there would be a specific theme to the event. Like Bénévent's observation of local sheep-rearing and its related industries, these could include such delights as celebrating the potato and the apple, in the latter case necessitating the consumption of large amounts of "cidre". The Donkey fair, "Fête du pain", Marching-band festival, Stamp and Postcard Collector Convention, "Bal Dansant", Open air Concert – each event contributed to life's rich tapestry in the summer months. They also provided an ideal opportunity to link up with friends and neighbours.

One of our favourite Foires was held in our nearby village of Vieilleville, where they held an annual display of vintage French cars, ancient military vehicles and traditional agricultural machinery, including working demonstrations.

This event particularly sticks in our minds, as a couple of months previously we had purchased an old farm plough as a display centrepiece in our garden, but it was missing its original wooden handles.

Off we went to Vieilleville.

"We may come across some handles for our plough there" we said in jest. As we turned the first corner into the main square, there before us was a stall selling a hotchpotch of old farm implements.

"You won't believe this," Chris said, "but I think they've got the exact pair of handles we are looking for, down beside that stall". After some haggling and quibbling, we bought them for ten euros. We were astonished to find when we got home and laid them onto our plough that they fitted exactly.

On one other occasion we set out to try to find a traditional oak table for our new lounge-dining room extension. We went to a huge brocante at Ambazac, a small town not far from Limoges. As we strolled towards the town centre, we noticed one trader selling furniture. We went over and there was exactly what we were searching for – an old oak circular table with two drop leaves, very worn and battered, but that only added to its charm. We approached the vendor, trying not to appear too excited.

"C'est combien , Madame?"

"150 euros"

Off on the haggling trail again.

"But it needs a lot of work."

"Agreed, but it is a very old table and still very beautiful."

"And it's got woodworm!"

"But it has been treated. The woodworm are all dead."

And so the exchanges continued until we settled on the price of 100 euros, sealing the deal with a handshake.

Now we had a problem. Our car was parked half a mile away and this was some heavy piece of furniture!

"Est-ce qu'il y a un problème?" the stallholder asked.

"Elle est très lourde"(it's very heavy) we replied.

Then with a booming voice that nearly deafened us, "Henri!" she called over to one of the two stewards standing nearby, who were sporting fluorescent yellow waistcoats.

"Henri, viens ici!" she bellowed. Henri came over at the double.

"Porte la table à la voiture pour Monsieur".

Henri took one look at the solid oak table and beckoned his colleague over.

Then, both standing to attention and saluting our "vendeuse" in mock obedience, they hoisted the table aloft and followed us through the crowds. They carried it the whole half-mile to the car, and even helped us to load it into the boot. We offered to pay them for their efforts and said we really appreciated their help.

"De rien" they said beaming, declining our offer of payment. "We are here today to help our community. Thank you for coming here and supporting us". With that they shook hands, turned, and made their way back to their post.

Car-boots have become a way of life in France, but near the end of our time there we learned that there were going to be new regulations coming in that would regulate the selling by private individuals. The reason behind this change was that many French and English people were making craft goods and artefacts then selling them at brocantes without having a permit to do so. They were therefore not paying tax on this activity. This was deemed unfair by the full-time traders who depended on this type of selling for their livelihood and who had to pay their taxes in full.

We visited one small village brocante after we became aware of the new regulations, and met an English lady who we had seen at several previous boot sales.

We got chatting and asked her how things were going, and she suddenly seemed close to tears.

"Is everything alright," we asked "can we be of any help?"

"Thank you," she replied "but there's nothing you or anyone can do. I've been here on my own now for several years, and to supplement my income I've been buying and selling at the car boot sales every summer. The money I've made has helped me to survive here through the winter, particularly last year with the drop in the value of the pound. I was just about getting by. It now appears that I will only be allowed to do a few boot sales each summer, and that will be a disaster for me."

We had arrived there quite late, but she told us that the gendarmes had visited all the stalls earlier in the day, and had explained that, in future, everyone would have to register their name and address with the brocante organiser. The details would then be forwarded to a central database where every participant would be checked.

We fully sympathised with her predicament, having ourselves been severely affected by the poor exchange rate in recent months. At the same time, we also recognised that it was essential to protect the jobs of full-time, fully registered traders and craftsmen.

We always found local brocantes and Foires entertaining, especially when they had marching bands in attendance. These added a whole new enjoyment to the experience especially with the variation in the quality of the music. Some of it was exceptionally good and some had to be heard to be believed, with renditions that owed more to gusto and enthusiasm than to talent. What united them all was the fun, vitality and sheer enjoyment they brought to the event.

Another feature that we remember with great fondness was watching entrepreneurial children trying to sell off their toys and games. On one occasion we stopped to buy a box of Lego, as one of the grandchildren was about to visit.

"I've got a castle and some soldiers as well" Antoine, all of seven years old, declared.

How did we know he was called Antoine? Well, displayed over his stall was a little hand-painted banner with "Antoine's toys" on it.

"But our grandson isn't two yet."

Diving down behind his stall, he reappeared clutching a battered plastic trike.

"Ten euros, and that's a bargain!"

"We could buy a new one for that!"

He paused for thought. "OK, it's yours for two euros!"

We took it, as a reward for his persistence. As we walked away following the deal, we both agreed, "That boy will go far".

We are not sure just how many brocantes we visited in our time in France. Peter had one particular item he would seek out at every single one, and that was screwdrivers.

"I never seem to be able to find the right one for the job when I need it" he would declare.

"Oh, you're not buying another bloody screwdriver" Chris would moan, "you've already got more than Brico Leclerc! We'll soon be able to open a shop with them".

"A slight exaggeration!"

Peter discovered, whilst sorting through his tools, that he had actually accumulated over one hundred assorted screwdrivers.

"You never know – they might come in useful."

It is probably wise not to record Chris's reply.

However, every visitor for the next few weeks was presented with a little screwdriver set without ever knowing why.

Lessons Learned the Hard Way

The screwdrivers, along with many accumulated specialist tools enabled both of us to develop an entirely new range of DIY skills. Some of these were taught to us by local artisans, some by English friends, some we acquired by trial and error.

After the "Acte de Vente" was signed, making us the legal owners of our little French house, we immediately began the restoration work that would be necessary to make it habitable.

From 2002 onwards we worked relentlessly on two fronts. In Birmingham, we were carrying out renovations room by room in order to update and upgrade the property. This work accelerated when we later decided to put it up for sale and move permanently to France. We also used every holiday break to drive over to Bénévent to work on the house there. This dual work continued until we emigrated in late September 2006.

After we relocated to France, as we outlined in "Pooh là là", we had the unenviable task of installing the septic tank pipework ourselves. Strangely enough we enjoyed this challenge, as we felt it was allowing us to get fitter whilst giving us a tremendous sense of achievement.

What we were not aware of at this stage was the damage all this work was doing to our health. In the early summer of 2007 Peter was working outside on a ladder, using a hammer drill while constructing a wood store. Without any warning he suddenly lost all the use in his left arm, dropping the drill which went crashing to the ground.

After an emergency appointment with our excellent GP, he was admitted within days to a hospital in Limoges where he spent a week undergoing a wide range of tests. The final diagnosis ruled out our greatest fear, that it could have been a stroke. The consultant told us that, quite simply, Peter's body was utterly worn out from too much DIY and not enough rest. It was imperative, he said, that he did nothing for the next three months.

When we got back home we tried to take stock of what had happened, and we knew the consultant was right. Slowly, and sticking to his advice and a total change of tempo, Peter recovered the use of his left arm. He had been warned not to try to use power tools for several months. He did make one exception to this rule when he used the drill to make holes in the garden to plant the winter cabbages! Solange, whose vegetable patch bordered ours, watched this unique method of planting in utter astonishment, laughingly telling us that in all her years of gardening, she had never seen anything quite like it. The crazy English!

However, in the late autumn, we fell into the trap loosely labelled by the expats as "the emptiness of the winter season in rural France". By late October everything closed down, leaving the lush green landscape bleak and bare. The long, cold and, frequently wet, days left everyone trapped indoors for extended periods of time over several months.

So how do you pass the time every day, apart from occasional shopping trips and visits to friends? Since moving to the Creuse, we had both become involved in outside activities in the region. Peter regularly attended a multi-faith discussion group in a village some 10 kilometres away, and also a writers' group that met in Aubusson, which was a 100-kilometre round trip. Chris was an active member of the local branch of Cancer Support, and also belonged to an association in Bénévent which was instrumental in installing a magnificent pipe organ in the twelfth-century Abbey, and arranging concerts there. We also both attended activities organised by the excellent English Library in La Souterraine, including an Anglo-French conversation group. However, in the depths of winter, when the roads were often treacherous, and with the increasing limitations imposed by our health problems, it often became difficult to travel the long distances required to pursue these activities.

So what did we do? Surprise, surprise! We carried on with home improvements. Accepting some physical limitations, and disregarding the words of our consultant, we merrily continued with the painting and decorating. There was a quiet celebration as we completed each room, accompanied by a nagging feeling that we should really be taking more rest.

Over the next two years all our time and energy, not to mention our financial resources, were directed to the addition of a new room that was built on the side of the house. This extension gave us a further living room downstairs. The project took up every moment of our time. It had been our resolution in the summer months that, when it ended, we would take a break from the work to explore new areas of France. This intention again went out of the window, as we focused all our energies on the DIY resulting from the new-build, and additional work to re-establish the garden that had been largely destroyed by the building work. Our flower garden and "potager" had been, after all, our pride and joy.

Unseen, invisibly, with us not having heeded the warning signs, we were, in fact, sitting on a ticking health time bomb.

In the summer of 2008, while a close friend was over on a visit, Chris tripped whilst weeding the rockery and fell against an ancient grinding wheel we had put in the garden as a decorative feature, fracturing two ribs. This took a considerable time to heal. Shortly afterwards she had to go into hospital for major surgery, which again required a long period of recovery.

By this time Peter had already sustained permanent damage in his throat, caused by a particular piece of building work.

We had spent two very productive months rebuilding and restoring a high stone boundary wall. Our neighbours in the hamlet even jokingly nicknamed us, "Les maçons de la Creuse" after the legendary stonemasons from the region who were responsible for constructing many of the famous buildings in Paris. The final stages of this work entailed lifting very heavy stones to be set on top of the restored wall. No one ever told us that, unless you had been a builder all your life, you should never lift heavy stones above shoulder height. Within three months of finishing this work Peter found it was becoming more and more difficult to swallow, and he was experiencing constant pain in his throat.

He was referred to a specialist who diagnosed that he now had a hiatus hernia at the base of his throat, most likely caused by all the heavy lifting. Since that time he has been on permanent medication to prevent acid reflux coming up from the stomach. This was one injury that could so easily have been avoided.

This would have been the right moment to stop completely and consider booking a long holiday. But there is something addictive about the process of bringing a house back to life that works its way under the skin. During the early summer a contractor had plasterboarded our loft and it needed painting. After receiving two expensive quotes, we came to an inevitable conclusion that it would be far cheaper to do it ourselves. No matter that this would mean working with extender-rollers, lying on planks on platforms, bending into very awkward nooks and crannies and kneeling for long periods on wooden floorboards, squeezed into the constricted space under the eaves. We were good at DIY; we could do it.

The holiday option flew out of the window; the materials and paint were purchased and we were off again. Altogether it took nearly two months to complete preparation and apply the two coats needed. The work became more and more taxing, often leaving us feeling exhausted – in fact, in simple terms, clapped out! Once it was completed, we stood back and admired our handiwork, thinking how great it was that we had saved so much money.

But the time bomb was still ticking away, and was close to exploding. Winter closed in and we knew it was too late to go away on holiday. Another opportunity missed. As the weeks passed we became more and more aware of how tired we were feeling and our reserves of energy seemed to be draining away.

On the evening of March 6th, 2009, we went up to bed as normal, with no inkling of what was about to happen. During that night the bomb exploded.

When Peter awoke the following morning, he was in utter agony. He had trapped nerves from his spine, the back of his neck, and along the whole of his left arm. If he moved his head in the slightest, the pain was excruciating. Somehow he managed to struggle downstairs before collapsing on the settee in agony, and calling out to Chris for help.

As she rushed downstairs, and before even being able to get to him, she blacked out, falling to the ground. It was impossible for either of us to help the other. Chris came round, but blacked out twice more, each time falling onto the tiled floor.

Eventually we were able to get to the phone and ring our neighbours for help.

We owed a massive debt to all the French doctors, consultants and specialists who treated us over the following weeks. They could not have been more caring and supportive through the course of many long and tiring examinations. We particularly appreciated the time they took at the end of each consultation to sit down with us and explain all the results, providing us with written reports, together with copies of our X-rays and scans.

The outcome was that Chris was unable to drive for nearly six months whilst undergoing medical tests, and spent a very long period recovering. For Peter it was nearly four weeks before a very gifted French physiotherapist could release the nerve trapped in the spine, and it took several months to free the left arm. By the time this happened, the left muscle had atrophied. As a result, he had virtually no use in the arm for nearly twelve months. Now, over three years later, the left hand still remains damaged.

In the long months of being forced to remain inactive for so many hours of the day, we came to realise what work on the house had really cost us — our health. The one thing that can never have a price put upon it.

It is impossible to put into words the debt of gratitude that we owed to a wide circle of friends and neighbours who came to our aid during these months. Jenny and Pete, very close friends, took care of our dog, Beau, for two weeks when we were both too ill to exercise him. So many meals were brought round, so many people took time to come and see us, and drove us to medical appointments and to collect prescriptions. They helped with shopping, washing, ironing, dog-walking, gardening, wood-stacking – the list could go on and on. At the time of our greatest need they became angels of mercy.

The only people who could not come to our aid were, of course, our children back in England. They felt this helplessness very deeply. There was no way that any of them, with work and family commitments could fly out and provide the ongoing help and support we were needing by this stage.

After resolutely trying to cope for a further two years we came to the heartbreaking decision that we could no longer continue our life in rural France. Our physical limitations meant that we could not manage the garden in summer and the vital task of woodcutting throughout the winter. One freezing January morning, when the pain for Peter had left him immobile, and Chris, on crutches following a further fall doing DIY, was trying to bring logs for the wood-burner into the house in a bucket, we reluctantly admitted that the situation was unsustainable.

We decided there were only two choices: either to move to another house in France, probably a more modern property with a much smaller garden, and access to public transport, or to move back to England. Knowing how the children still struggled with being unable to help us, we took the difficult decision to return to England.

At a time of national recession, and with a slump in the property market, we miraculously sold our home in France in two weeks, simply by fixing a home-made "À Vendre" sign on the garden gate. The purchase of our new home in England, found via the internet, was completed in just over a month.

Another quiet miracle?

As we drove away from the hamlet on 11th May 2011, with tears in our eyes, our neighbours came to wave us goodbye.

"Au revoir, nos amis, et bon courage!"

We will treasure forever the four-and-a-half years we spent in France, living our dream, with so many wonderful memories and so many great friends.

But our regret is massive. It could all have been so different if we had taken everything at a far slower pace. We never took advantage of all the holidays that were there on our doorstep. So many lost opportunities! We missed seeing so much of the richness, beauty, variety and vitality of other regions of France. We could have preserved our health and well-being if we had only done things in easy stages.

We learned our lesson the hard way. It is our hope, in including this final story in the collection, that others who are thinking of making the same journey may be helped to tread a different, and hopefully far wiser, path.

Acknowledgements

I would like to thank the members of the Rubery Writers' Group, who meet every fortnight at Rubery Library, for all their support, challenge, friendship and encouragement in spurring me on to become a writer.

After submitting some early short stories to different competitions this spring, it was a thrilling surprise to be contacted in late April by "Writing Magazine" to say that I had won the competition they jointly run with "Skyros Holidays".

The winning story "Happiness is a wardrobe slowly rising in the air" is published in this collection.

I talked over with Chris the possibility of writing further stories of similar experiences. We knew there were many. After considerable discussion, and urged on by family and friends we took the decision to co-write "Bon Courage Les Anglais".

Our deep thanks go to Liz Obee for her editorial work on the book. We especially appreciated her perceptive observations without which we may have left our readers in a state of confusion.

We also express our thanks to Fifi Sharplin for accepting our commission to provide the illustrations. We feel they capture so perfectly the spirit of each story. We thank her for her hard work, dedication and enthusiasm, and to her husband Tim for his support.

We know this book could never have been produced without the help and expertise of the team at PublishNation.

In drawing to a close, we accept that, if there are any errors or omissions, these are entirely our responsibility.

Peter and Christine Wakefield

August 2012.

Printed in Great Britain
by Amazon.co.uk, Ltd.,
Marston Gate.